Reading Comprehension Skills and Strategies

Level 7

Saddleback Publishing, Inc.
Three Watson
Irvine, CA 92618-2767
E-Mail: info@sdlback.com
Web site: www.sdlback.com

Development and Production:
The EDGe

ISBN 1-56254-034-3

Printed in the United States of America
06 05 04   9 8 7 6 5 4 3 2

Table of Contents
Skills

About this Series

This unique series is specially created for you by Saddleback Publishing, Inc., as an exciting supplement to reinforce and extend your classroom reading curriculum. *Reading Comprehension Skills and Strategies* can easily be integrated into basic reading curricula as additional reading lessons: as stand-alone strategy and skill instructional lessons; as across-the-curriculum lessons; or as activities for students with special projects, interests, or abilities.

This series is based on the most current research and thought concerning the teaching of reading comprehension. This series not only sharpens traditional reading comprehension skills (main idea, story plot, topic sentence, sequencing, etc.), but it also reinforces the critical reading comprehension strategies that encourage your students to use prior knowledge, experiences, careful thought, and evaluation to help them decide how to practically apply what they know to all reading situations.

Traditional comprehension skills recently have been woven into the larger context of strategy instruction. Today, literacy instruction emphasizes learning strategies—those approaches that coordinate the various reading and writing skills and prior knowledge to make sense to the learner. Our goal in this series is to provide you and your students with the most up-to-date reading comprehension support, while teaching basic skills that can be tested and evaluated.

Reading Comprehension Strategies

- vocabulary knowledge
- activating prior knowledge
- pre-reading—previewing and predicting
- previewing and predicting text
- mental imaging
- self-questioning
- summarizing
- semantic mapping

Saddleback Publishing, Inc., promotes the development of the whole child with particular emphasis on combining solid skill instruction with creativity and imagination. This series gives your students a variety of opportunities to apply reading comprehension strategies as they read, while reinforcing basic reading comprehension skills. In addition, we designed this series to help you make an easy transition between levels (grades 6, 7, and 8) in order to reinforce or enhance needed skill development for individual students.

About this Book

Reading Comprehension Skills and Strategies is designed to reinforce and extend the reading skills of your students. The fun, high-interest fiction and non-fiction selections will spark the interest of even your most reluctant reader. The book offers your students a variety of reading opportunities—reading for pleasure, reading to gather information, and reading to perform a task. Characters throughout the book prompt the student to apply one of the strategies to the reading selection and includes a relevant comprehension skill activity.

Choosing Instructional Approaches

You can use the pages in this book for independent reinforcement or extension, whole group lessons, pairs, or small cooperative groups rotating through an established reading learning center. You may choose to place the activities in a center and reproduce the answer key for self-checking. To ensure the utmost flexibility, the process for managing this is left entirely up to you because you know what works best in your classroom.

Assessment

Assessment and evaluation of student understanding and ability is an ongoing process. A variety of methods and strategies should be used to ensure that the student is being assessed and evaluated in a fair and comprehensive manner. Always keep in mind that the assessment should take into consideration the opportunities the student had to learn the information and practice the skills presented. The strategies for assessment are left for you to determine and are dependent on your students and your particular instructional plan. You will find a Scope & Sequence chart at the back of this book to assist you as you develop your assessment plan.

Directions: *Answer each question. Be able to explain the reason for your answer.*

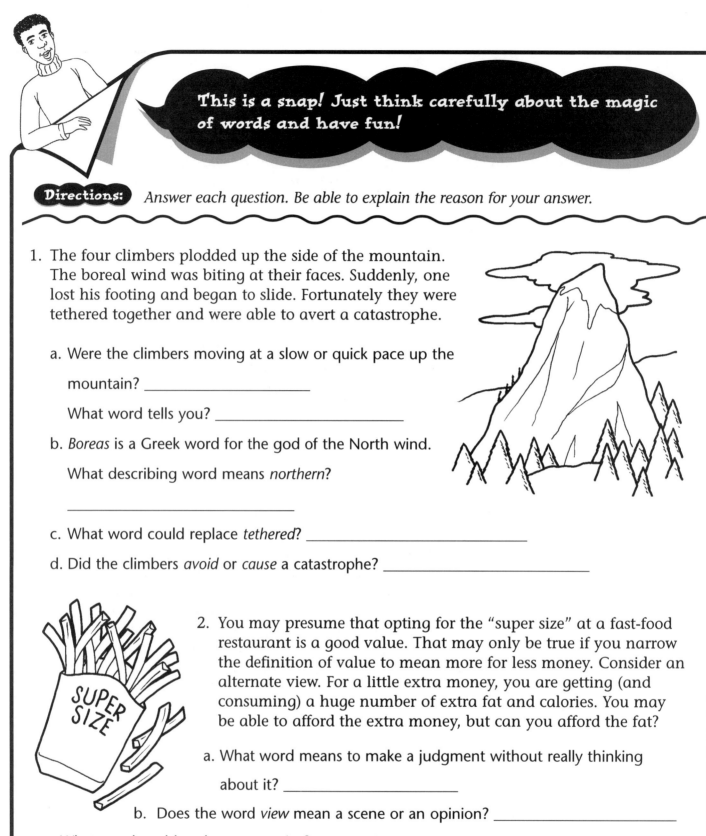

1. The four climbers plodded up the side of the mountain. The boreal wind was biting at their faces. Suddenly, one lost his footing and began to slide. Fortunately they were tethered together and were able to avert a catastrophe.

   a. Were the climbers moving at a slow or quick pace up the mountain? _____

   What word tells you? _____

   b. *Boreas* is a Greek word for the god of the North wind. What describing word means *northern*?

   _____

   c. What word could replace *tethered*? _____

   d. Did the climbers *avoid* or *cause* a catastrophe? _____

2. You may presume that opting for the "super size" at a fast-food restaurant is a good value. That may only be true if you narrow the definition of value to mean more for less money. Consider an alternate view. For a little extra money, you are getting (and consuming) a huge number of extra fat and calories. You may be able to afford the extra money, but can you afford the fat?

   a. What word means to make a judgment without really thinking about it? _____

   b. Does the word *view* mean a scene or an opinion? _____

   c. What word could replace *consuming*? _____

   d. What word means *bear the cost* or *consequences*? _____

   e. What consequences might the writer of this passage be warning you of? _____

   _____

Name: _____ **Date:** _____

1. While eating, a lion will often _____ to lick its _____.

| **paws**: animal feet |
| **pause**: brief stop |

2. The family lived in a royal _____ on a large _____.

| **manner**: style |
| **manor**: estate |

3. Our team is ahead because we _____ _____ more game than the next team.

| **one**: number 1 |
| **won**: past of win |

4. My puppy _____ shoes, but he always seems to _____ mine.

| **choose**: pick |
| **chews**: bites |

5. Her _____ carried her to the finish of the marathon—quite a _____!

| **feat**: accomplishment |
| **feet**: plural of foot |

6. He had to _____ someone to replace him because he took a _____ position.

| **hire**: employ |
| **higher**: above |

7. I will _____ the amount of homework if you give full attention to the _____.

| **lesson**: instruction |
| **lessen**: make less |

8. The _____, where Congress meets, is located in the nation's _____.

| **capital**: a city |
| **capitol**: a building |

9. The _____ aren't done yet because I forgot to _____ the door of the dryer.

| **close**: shut |
| **clothes**: clothing |

Name: _____ **Date:** _____

It's really fun to change the meaning of words by adding different prefixes and suffixes.

- proved to be false or unbelievable
- a structure for transporting water
- a reason to move or take action
- to brighten or enlighten
- a set of names or system of naming
- one who is new at doing something
- to please, calm, or make peace
- someone who watches

1. If **luminous** means giving off light or brightness, then **illuminate** means

_____

2. If a **spectacle** is something to watch, then a **spectator** is

_____

3. If **credible** means able to be believed, then **discredit** means

_____

4. If **placid** means peaceful and calm, then **placate** means

_____

5. If **nominate** means to name, appoint, or identify, then a **nomenclature** is

_____

6. If an **aquarium** is a water environment, then an **aqueduct** is

_____

7. If **mobile** means capable of moving, then **motivation** means

_____

Name: _____ Date: _____

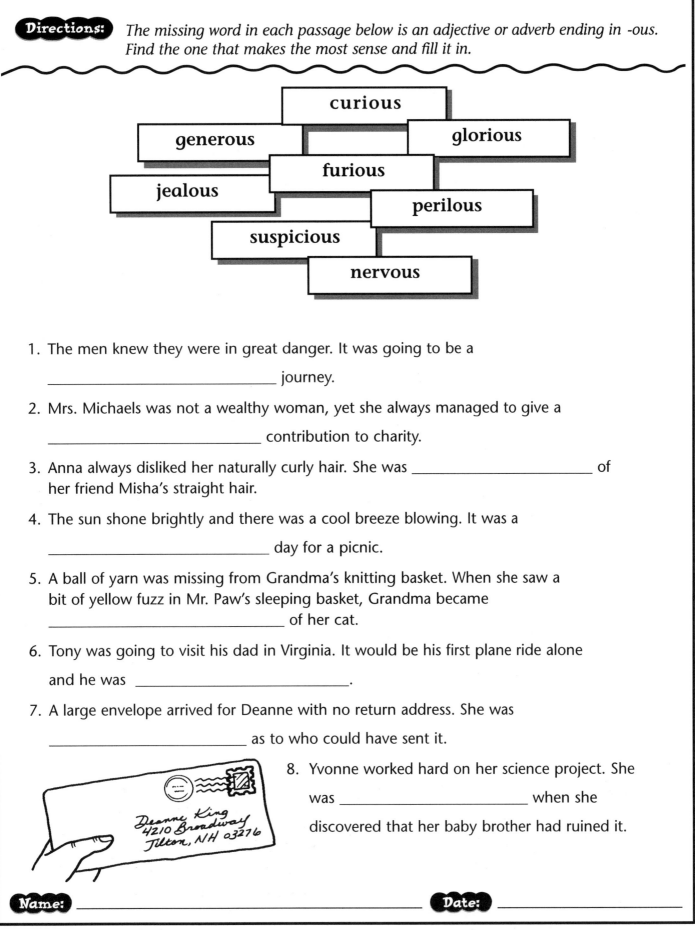

curious

generous

glorious

furious

jealous

perilous

suspicious

nervous

1. The men knew they were in great danger. It was going to be a

_____ journey.

2. Mrs. Michaels was not a wealthy woman, yet she always managed to give a

_____ contribution to charity.

3. Anna always disliked her naturally curly hair. She was _____ of her friend Misha's straight hair.

4. The sun shone brightly and there was a cool breeze blowing. It was a

_____ day for a picnic.

5. A ball of yarn was missing from Grandma's knitting basket. When she saw a bit of yellow fuzz in Mr. Paw's sleeping basket, Grandma became

_____ of her cat.

6. Tony was going to visit his dad in Virginia. It would be his first plane ride alone

and he was _____.

7. A large envelope arrived for Deanne with no return address. She was

_____ as to who could have sent it.

8. Yvonne worked hard on her science project. She was _____ when she discovered that her baby brother had ruined it.

Name: _____   **Date:** _____

encouragement	statement	commitment	postponement
fulfillment	retirement	adjournment	detriment

1. We had to move the party to a later date. I was disappointed at the

   _____.

2. Mrs. Long had been a teacher for 30 years. She was looking forward to her

   _____.

3. The runner finally achieved what he had always wanted. Winning the gold medal was the

   _____ of all his dreams.

4. Dad had always assured me that I could do it.
   I appreciated his

   _____.

5. The club meeting was over and the leader
   called for an

   _____.

6. On the basketball court, being undersized is a

   _____.

7. I knew that having a paper route meant getting up early and
   always getting the job done. I was willing to make the

   _____.

8. When asked if he would run for office again, rather than answering right away, the Mayor
   prepared a written _____.

Name: _____   **Date:** _____

- praise given as a result of an action
- to carry or bring in
- able to act independently
- to leave or empty out
- able to use both hands with equal skill
- one who is new at doing something
- to enact into law
- one that resists; enemy

1. If **ambi**valence means having two opposing feelings, then **ambi**dextrous means

_____

2. If **port**able means able to be carried, then im**port** means

_____

3. If **compli**ance is the act of fulfilling a requirement, then a **compli**ment is

_____

4. If **auto**matic means able to work on its own, then **auto**nomy means

_____

5. If **nov**el means new or not known before, then a **nov**ice is

_____

6. If il**leg**al means against the law, then **leg**islate means

_____

7. If **vac**ant means unoccupied or empty, then e**vac**uate means

_____

8. If **adverse** means opposed to one's interest, then **adversary** means

_____

Name: _____   **Date:** _____

What do you do many times every day of your life, often without even realizing it? Follow directions! It's important to keep this skill sharp!

Directions: *Your ability to read and follow directions carefully can be useful in many situations—anything from solving a puzzle to saving your life. Practice with this puzzle.*

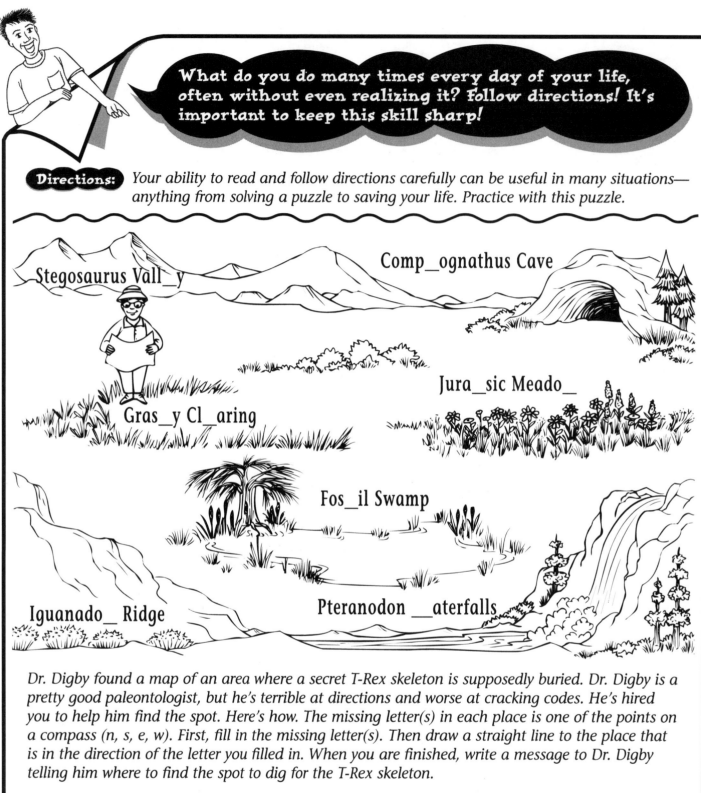

Stegosaurus Vall_y

Comp_ognathus Cave

Gras_y Cl_aring

Jura_sic Meado_

Fos_il Swamp

Iguanado_ Ridge

Pteranodon __aterfalls

Dr. Digby found a map of an area where a secret T-Rex skeleton is supposedly buried. Dr. Digby is a pretty good paleontologist, but he's terrible at directions and worse at cracking codes. He's hired you to help him find the spot. Here's how. The missing letter(s) in each place is one of the points on a compass (n, s, e, w). First, fill in the missing letter(s). Then draw a straight line to the place that is in the direction of the letter you filled in. When you are finished, write a message to Dr. Digby telling him where to find the spot to dig for the T-Rex skeleton.

_____

_____

_____

_____

Name: _____   **Date:** _____

Here's a puzzle to solve that takes concentration, a little knowledge, and the ability to follow directions. The solution is hidden in the grid. Color the box to indicate coordinates. Remember, to find a coordinate, move over, then up. For example, coordinate (8,B) is over 8, then up to B. Good luck!

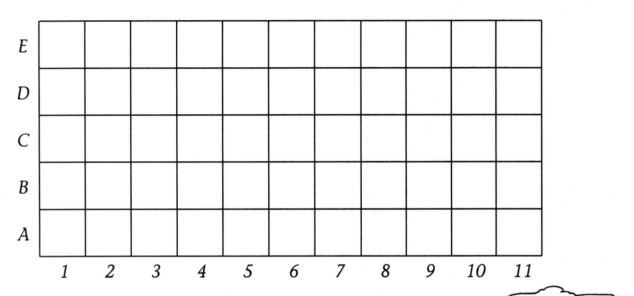

1. If penguins are found in the Arctic, color boxes (4,E) and (8,B) green.
   If penguins are not found in the Arctic, color boxes (1,E) and (10,C) red.

2. If the moon is not a planet, color boxes (3,E) (6,A) and (9,C) red.
   If the moon is a planet, color boxes (4,A) (8,E) and (9,B) green.

3. If a koala is a bear, color boxes (1,B) (7,C) and (11,D) yellow.
   If a koala is not a bear, color boxes (2,A) (6,C) (5,E) and (11,E) red.

4. If our atmosphere is mostly oxygen, color boxes (2,E) (8,A) and (4,C) green.
   If our atmosphere is not mostly oxygen, color boxes (6,E) (9,A) and (11,B) red.

5. If there are 48 states total in the United States, boxes (6,D) (3,B) and (8,D) yellow.
   If there are not 48 states total in the United States, color boxes (9,E) (2,D) and (5,C) red.

6. If a centimeter is longer than an inch, color boxes (6,B) (1,A) and (10,D) green.
   If a centimeter is not longer than an inch, color boxes (2,B) (7,E) and (5,A) red.

7. If the earth revolves around the sun, color boxes (10,E) (5,B) (1,D) and (11,A) red.
   If the earth does not revolve around the sun, color boxes (1,C) and (7,B) yellow.

8. If Egypt is in Africa, color boxes (9,D) (7,A) and (2,C) red.
   If Egypt is not in Africa, color boxes (8,C) (3,A) and (4,D) green.

9. If the number 1 million has 6 zeros, color boxes (3,D) (11,C) (5,D) and (10,A) red.
   If the number 1 million does not have 6 zeros, color boxes (3,C) (4,B) and (10,B) yellow.

To find out how well you did, what do you see on the grid and in what color?

_____

Name: _____ **Date:** _____

Directions: *Use context clues to figure out the meaning of the bold word. Write it on the line.*

1. The restaurant on the dock had a **nautical** theme.

   _____

2. That criticism was a **crass** remark.

   _____

3. The old tree's trunk was **gnarled**.

   _____

4. I had a **hunch** that you would show up today.

   _____

5. We will **implement** the plan according to schedule.

   _____

6. I heard the noisy chatter of a **magpie**.

   _____

7. Some snakes are **oviparous**; others give live birth.

   _____

8. At last we spotted a **pod** of whales.

   _____

9. "I saw it first," Stan **quipped**.

   _____

10. The party put us in a **jovial** mood.

    _____

11. The inexpensive jewelry contained **faux** gems.

    _____

12. She has an **aptitude** for solving problems.

    _____

- small group
- twisted and knotty
- related to ships or sailing
- egg-producing
- happy, cheerful
- rude, insensitive
- remarked
- put into effect
- fake, artificial
- gut feeling, premonition
- natural ability, talent
- a jaylike bird

Name: _____   **Date:** _____

Today was the day Jamal had dreamed about for most of his 22 years. As he stood in the tunnel waiting for the **profound** moment when he would first step out on the field, he thought about how he had arrived at this point.

He smiled fondly at the mental picture of himself as a nine-year-old in an oversized uniform. He recalled falling **intermittently** and **fumbling** the too-big ball. Middle school was better, but still he made mistakes and a few times even cost his team the game. In high school, he **toiled** long hours to get into top physical shape and then **crammed** his nose into the books to keep his grades high. It had paid off. He made it into a good college on a football scholarship. Day in and day out, he studied, worked out, and practiced. The **scouts** took notice of him, and when draft day came he waited nervously through a **litany** of names until, yes, his was **ultimately** called. Third-round choice—the fourth running back chosen overall.

The summer had been hot and **grueling**. Not only did he endure the exhaustion of pushing his body to the limits in team practices and his mind into learning dozens of formations in the team's playbook, but he also took the **razzing** that veteran players dish out to rookies, and the anxiety of possibly being cut from the team.

But, here he was. The first game of the regular season. Just moments ago he had **donned** his pads and proudly put on his uniform. As the crowd noise **swelled**, so did his heart. He had made it onto a professional football team.

1. extremely difficult and tiresome: _____

2. reciting of a list: _____

3. finally; at last; in the end: _____

4. worked hard: _____

5. teasing; playing pranks on: _____

6. put on or dressed in: _____

7. rose; grew in size or strength: _____

8. periodically; from time to time: _____

9. pushed; placed with intensity: _____

10. people who search for those with particular talents: _____

11. handling clumsily; dropping; loosing grip: _____

12. deeply or intensely felt: _____

Name: _____   Date: _____

Directions: *Here's a fun way for you to see how well you use context clues. Solve the puzzle by filling in the term that could take the place of the bold word in each clue. The answers you need (and some you don't) are in the box.*

ACROSS
2. The earthquake caused a **fissure** in the ground's surface.
4. They were able to **salvage** usable parts from the old car.
5. We knew from the **onset** what was coming.
6. The police **interrogated** all the witnesses.
8. My cat has a **peculiar** trait—six toes on each foot!
10. He was a **shrewd** chess player.
11. Wearing a seat belt can help you **avert** injury.

DOWN
1. Dr. Cha is a scientist of **eminence** in his field.
2. The unclear directions left me **muddled**.
3. The animals stayed clear of the lion's known **turf**.
7. He could barely **utter** a word.
9. They began to **excavate** the site with picks and shovels.

HELP BOX
crack
questioned
bury
odd
dig
clever
distinction
muddy
save
land
end
avoid
confused
speak
territory
silly
beginning

Name: _____   Date: _____

Directions: *Finish each sentence with the word that correctly completes it.*

1. Cal raised it over his head, then slammed it hard against the nail. Cal was using a

_____.

2. Cal looked at the menu. "What is available for vegetarians?" he asked the waiter. "I don't eat

_____."

3. Cal took his wife and two children to the park for a baseball game. Cal is

_____.

4. Cal and his son watched as the player shot the puck into the net. They were watching

_____.

5. Cal drives an 18-wheel big rig up and down the interstate, delivering fresh fruits and vegetables. Cal is a

_____.

6. Mrs. Rowe had three children—Cal, Jess, and Rose. Mrs. Rowe is John's mother and Rose is Cal's

_____.

Name: _____   Date: _____

1. Charlie and Nan had to pedal hard to make it up the steep hill.

   What were they riding?

   O skateboards
   O bikes
   O can't tell

2. The sweet scents coming from Mrs. Olsen's kitchen were irresistible.

   What was Mrs. Olsen making?

   O cookies
   O pies
   O can't tell

3. Thousands stood up and cheered when the ball went into the net.

   What sport were they watching?

   O hockey
   O basketball
   O can't tell

4. "Look," said Tammy, "This little candy bar has 280 calories!"

   What was Tammy looking at?

   O the label on a wrapper
   O a window advertisement
   O can't tell

5. On the way to pick up Dad, Tim asked, "What time does he land?"

   How was Dad arriving?

   O by train
   O by plane
   O can't tell

6. Denise looked at the grade on her math test and grimaced.

   What kind of grade did Denise get?

   O higher than expected
   O lower than expected
   O can't tell

7. Kevin examined its delicate wings. "I think its injured," he said.

   What was Kevin holding?

   O a butterfly
   O a baby bird
   O can't tell

8. David beamed when his big sister let him use her new computer game.

   How did David feel?

   O delighted
   O disappointed
   O can't tell

9. Sabrina said, "Lettuce and tomato, but no mayonnaise, please."

   What was Sabrina buying?

   O a pizza
   O a sandwich
   O can't tell

Directions: *Words with multiple meanings can trip you up. Try your hand with the ones below. Read the various meanings for each word. Write the number of the correct meaning.*

stand 1. to place in a vertical position 2. to stay in a specific position or condition; rank 3. an opinion 4. to stay in effect 5. to endure 6. to undertake or perform duty

1. Where does the team stand in the playoffs? #_____

2. She couldn't stand the screeching noise. #_____

3. Please stand for the flag salute. #_____

4. Dad said his decision will stand. #_____

5. What is your stand on the issue? #_____

6. He will stand guard at the outpost. #_____

7. The ladder would hold up to 200 pounds. #_____

8. Will the weather hold for the weekend? #_____

9. The city will hold a meeting about traffic. #_____

10. Will you hold this for me for a minute? #_____

11. The speaker had a hold on the audience. #_____

12. Does this jar hold 16 ounces? #_____

13. The baggage was placed in the hold. #_____

14. The wall did not hold back the water. #_____

15. The soldiers were able to hold the fort. #_____

16. We put a hold on our mail during vacation. #_____

17. I hold the view that recycling is important. #_____

18. Will the old roof hold in a windstorm? #_____

hold 1. to have or keep in one's possession 2. to restrain or limit 3. to support 4. to contain 5. to have in mind, as in an idea 6. to carry on a group action, as in a meeting 7. to last or remain 8. to influence 9. part of a ship for storing cargo 10. to temporarily stop

Name: _____

Date: _____

Directions: *You already know an amazing number of words, but you continuously increase your word power by adding new words you encounter to your vocabulary. You may or may not know the words below. Use a dictionary to help you with the ones you don't know.*

invoke
humane
insolent
solitude
gumption
covenant
paragon
allocate
augment
remedy
journal
frugal

What living lizard can grow up to 10 feet long and weigh 300 pounds?
To solve the puzzle, find the word above that matches each definition. Then write the word, one letter to a blank. Read the answer under the ★.

★

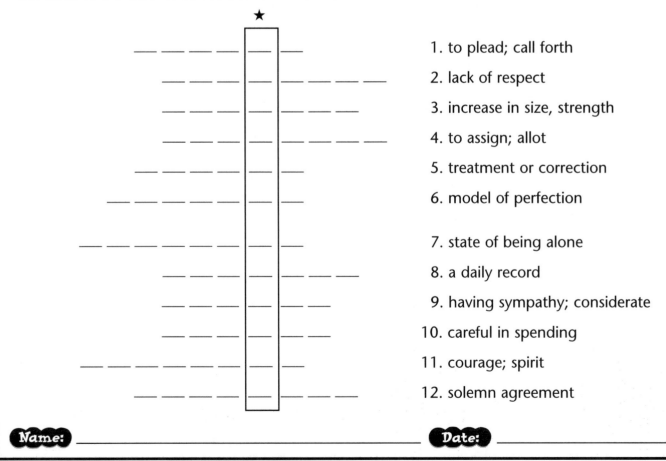

1. to plead; call forth

2. lack of respect

3. increase in size, strength

4. to assign; allot

5. treatment or correction

6. model of perfection

7. state of being alone

8. a daily record

9. having sympathy; considerate

10. careful in spending

11. courage; spirit

12. solemn agreement

Name: _____   **Date:** _____

Directions: *When encountering new words, a good strategy is to use what you already know. Is this word similar to one you are already familiar with? Try this strategy below. Follow the example to see how.*

The prisoner was led out in **manacles.**

A word like *manacles* that I already know is **manual**, which means __by hand__.

So, **manacles** probably means ☐ eyeglasses ☒ handcuffs/chains ☐ tentacles/arms

1. *She was one of the world's best known* **contemporary** *writers.*

   A word like *contemporary* that I already know is **temporary,**

   which means _____.

   So, **contemporary** probably means ☐ disliked ☐ famous ☐ of modern times

2. *The old* **mariner** *spoke wisely about the dangers we faced.*

   A word like *mariner* that I already know is **marine,**

   which means _____.

   So, **mariner** probably means ☐ sailor ☐ miner ☐ watchman

3. *The electricity was being generated by* **hydraulic** *energy.*

   A word like *hydraulic* that I already know is **hydrant,** as in fire hydrant,

   which means _____.

   So, **hydraulic** probably means ☐ raised ☐ water-powered ☐ hydrogen-powered

4. *The fire chief said the evidence was* **definitive.**

   A word like *definitive* that I already know is **finite,**

   which means _____.

   So, **definitive** probably means ☐ clearly stated ☐ final/conclusive ☐ questionable

Name: _____ Date: _____

Directions: *Read each statement, paying special attention to the boldfaced word or phrase. What message is it sending? Choose the best answer.*

1. Every year Wes asks for a chocolate cake for his birthday. **However**, this year...

   O there's more detail to come
   O an opposite idea is coming
   O these ideas are in order

2. Mrs. Washington assigned the class a report. "You are to include at least three different kinds of sources," she instructed. "**In addition**, you must..."

   O there's more detail to come
   O an opposite idea is coming
   O these ideas are in order

3. Dr. Taylor was silent as he examined my overweight cat. Then he looked at me and said, "**Although** he appears healthy now, this guy's weight..."

   O there's more detail to come
   O an opposite idea is coming
   O these ideas are in order

4. Merideth was obviously excited. She went right to the computer to e-mail Sally. **Earlier** she had heard the news. **Now**, she couldn't wait...

   O there's more detail to come
   O an opposite idea is coming
   O these ideas are in order

5. You probably imagine bears as slow, lumbering creatures. **In contrast**, bears can move very quickly for short distances.

   O there's more detail to come
   O an opposite idea is coming
   O these ideas are in order

6. Tom and Mike had been playing ball in the house against Mom's rules and broke a vase. They knew they were in trouble and **furthermore**...

   O there's more detail to come
   O an opposite idea is coming
   O these ideas are in order

7. Clay was down in the dumps. Art asked him why. "**For one thing**, I missed getting an A in math by two points. **Next**, ...

   O there's more detail to come
   O an opposite idea is coming
   O these ideas are in order

Reading Comprehension • Saddleback Publishing, Inc. ©2002   22   3 Watson, Irvine, CA 92618•Phone (888)SDL-BACK• www.sdlback.com

- as a result
- a key feature
- therefore
- rather
- the main point
- however
- in summary
- yet
- noteworthy
- in conclusion
- like; unlike
- most of all
- remember
- consequently
- but
- hence
- although
- principally

SIGNAL: An Important point is coming!

SIGNAL: A comparison is coming!

SIGNAL: A conclusion is coming!

Directions: In the speech bubbles are quotes from Carl's oral report on the Wright brothers. Use the clues to help you match the meaning of each bold word. Write the letter on the line. The first one is done for you as an example. Use a dictionary if needed.

_____ 1. in secret; out of public view

_____ 2. changes; improvements

__A__ 3. mocked; laughed

_____ 4. legal claim, title, or rights

_____ 5. ran; managed

_____ 6. money given for a purpose

_____ 7. experimented

_____ 8. in the air

(A) When Orville and Wilbur Wright first talked of flying they were **scoffed** at.

(B) In 1895, the Wright brothers **operated** a bicycle repair shop and a small plant for manufacturing bicycles.

(C) The brothers **tinkered** with ideas from gliders and the new gasoline buggies (cars) that were being developed.

(D) To avoid ridicule, Orville and Wilbur worked **stealthily** on their flying machine.

(E) The first real flight took place on December 17, 1903, when the Wright brothers' plane traveled 260 yards **aloft**.

(F) After many **moderations**, three years later Wilbur took their plane to France, where he made a flight of 52 miles in 92 minutes.

(G) After some setbacks, the brothers were able to get **appropriations** from Congress to continue their work.

(H) Eventually, the Wright brothers' **interests** were bought out by the Curtiss Company.

Name: _____

Date: _____

ACROSS

3. When accused, Sandy ____ taking the pencil. (denied / detailed)

5. A bat ____ on its hearing to navigate. (relieves / relies)

7. The sleeping cat was ____ by the loud noise. (startled / started)

8. The king put forth a ____ to the people. (degree / decree)

DOWN

1. The puppy ____ when she hurt her paw. (whispered / whimpered)

2. Lightning ____ the branch from the tree. (several / severed)

4. The boy's size ____ in comparison to the giant's. (paled / pulled)

6. The sailors ____ their gear in trunks. (stowe / stole)

9. The old man walked with a ____. (can / cane)

 Name: _____   Date: _____

aloft: up high   **alarm**: danger warning

shore: water's edge   **shall**: will

march: progress toward   **folk**: people

arm: prepare for defense   **signal**: notification

An Excerpt from "Paul Revere's Ride"
by Henry Wadsworth Longfellow

Listen, my children, and you _____ hear

of the midnight ride of Paul Revere,

on the eighteenth of April, in seventy-five;

hardly a man is now alive

who remembers that famous day and year.

He said to his friend, "If the British _____

by land or by sea from the town tonight

hang a lantern _____ in the belfry arch

of the North Church tower as a _____ light —

one, if by land, and two, if by sea;

and I on the opposite _____ will be,

ready to ride and spread the _____

through every Middlesex village and farm,

for the country _____ to be up and to _____.

Name: _____   Date: _____

The Sumatran Rhino

Of the five surviving species of rhinoceros, the Sumatran is the smallest. It is about 8-9 feet in length and weighs up to 1,700 pounds. Of its two horns, the front is the more prominent. It can be worn down but will regenerate even if broken. The upper lip is prehensile.

This rhino's facial skin is wrinkled, but the area around the muzzle is unwrinkled due to keratinization. Its body skin is rough and granular with a conspicuous fold behind the shoulders. In the young, coarse bristly hair is plentiful but diminishes with age.

The Sumatran rhino is surprisingly agile. It can climb thickly forested mountain sides—too steep for a man. Its poor vision is offset by its keen senses of smell and hearing. It is an elusive creature and is able to survive in rain forest areas practically impenetrable by man and other animals.

_____ 1. conspicuous   a. impossible to pass through, enter, or pierce

_____ 2. keratinization   b. clever or tricky in avoiding or escaping

_____ 3. agile   c. easy to see; readily apparent

_____ 4. impenetrable   d. brushlike; having short stiff hairs

_____ 5. regenerate   e. to form or grow back a lost part

_____ 6. bristly   f. hardening of protein, such as found in hair, skin

_____ 7. elusive   g. able to grasp things

_____ 8. prehensile   h. skillful in movement; quick or keen

Name: _____   **Date:** _____

Directions: Below is a schedule of activities offered at a local center for the performing arts. Use it to answer the questions below.

City Center for the Performing Arts

For tickets or information call 534-3967 or go to www.CityCentPerf.org

Sun.	Mon.	Tues.	Wed.	Thurs.	Fri.	Sat.
			1	**2** Dance for Wellness, a fundraiser for City Hospital 7pm. $20	**3** "The Big River" an historical play for the family. 8pm $8 adult, $4 child	**4** "The Big River"
5 "The Big River" matinee 2pm	**6** "Reading Rainbow" for ages 4-8, 4pm free (different each week)	**7** "You're a Good Man Charlie Brown" 4pm $2 donation	**8** "Reading Rainbow" for ages 4-8, 4pm free (different each week)	**9** "You're a Good Man Charlie Brown" 4pm $2 donation	**10**	**11**
12	**13** "Reading Rainbow" for ages 4-8, 4pm free (different each week)	**14**	**15** "Reading Rainbow" for ages 4-8, 4pm free (different each week)	**16**	**17** Los Cancioneros Master Chorale 7pm $15 adult $5 child	**18**
19 Durga Puja song and dance from India 7pm free	**20** "Reading Rainbow" for ages 4-8, 4pm free (different each week)	**21**	**22** "Reading Rainbow" for ages 4-8, 4pm free (different each week)	**23**	**24**	**25** Young Artists Gallery opens. Works on display through Nov. 30
26	**27** "Reading Rainbow" for ages 4-8, 4pm free (different each week)	**28**	**29** "Reading Rainbow" for ages 4-8, 4pm free (different each week)	**30**	**31** Police Dept.'s Annual Community Halloween Party 6 pm free	

1. For what month is this schedule? _____

2. Does the City Center for the Performing Arts have a Web site? _____

3. How many different Reading Rainbow presentations could a child attend? _____

4. What program is offered as an evening performance or a matinee? _____

5. What can be seen every day beginning on the 25th? _____

6. What special event is held every year? _____

7. Why do you think the weekday offerings are at 4 pm? _____

8. What would it cost for two adults and one child to see the Master Chorale? _____

Name: _____ **Date:** _____

How do you find people and services in your community? The phone book is still a good source. For Part 1, the phone book shown represents a combination of the white and yellow pages. Use it to answer the questions. For Part 2, use your real phone book.

A. *To what section would you go to first to find ....*

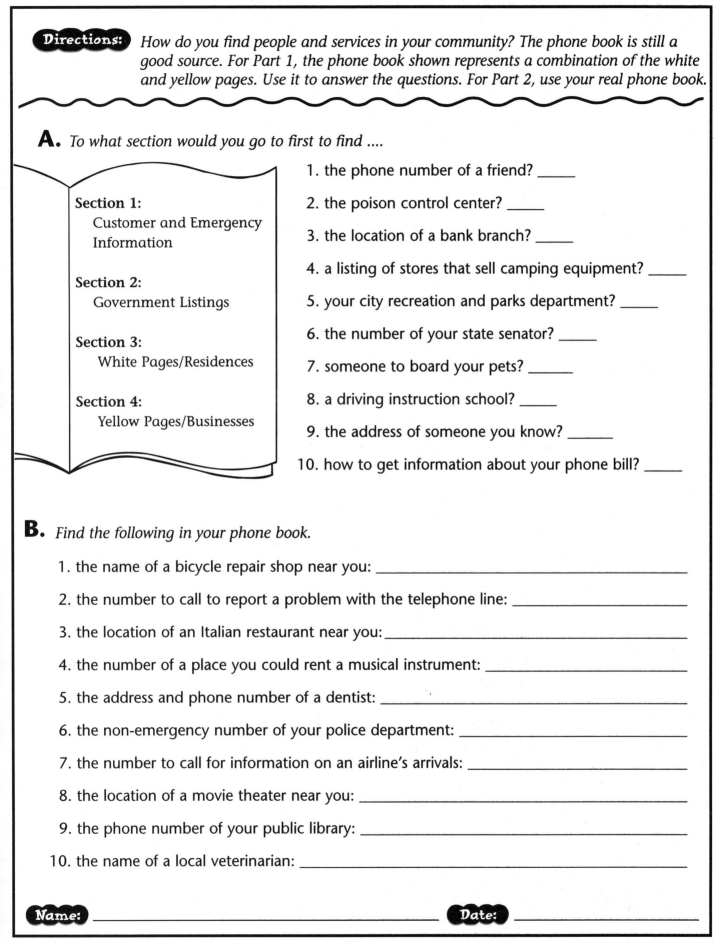

Section 1:
    Customer and Emergency
    Information

Section 2:
    Government Listings

Section 3:
    White Pages/Residences

Section 4:
    Yellow Pages/Businesses

1. the phone number of a friend? _____

2. the poison control center? _____

3. the location of a bank branch? _____

4. a listing of stores that sell camping equipment? _____

5. your city recreation and parks department? _____

6. the number of your state senator? _____

7. someone to board your pets? _____

8. a driving instruction school? _____

9. the address of someone you know? _____

10. how to get information about your phone bill? _____

B. *Find the following in your phone book.*

1. the name of a bicycle repair shop near you: _____

2. the number to call to report a problem with the telephone line: _____

3. the location of an Italian restaurant near you: _____

4. the number of a place you could rent a musical instrument: _____

5. the address and phone number of a dentist: _____

6. the non-emergency number of your police department: _____

7. the number to call for information on an airline's arrivals: _____

8. the location of a movie theater near you: _____

9. the phone number of your public library: _____

10. the name of a local veterinarian: _____

Name: _____   **Date:** _____

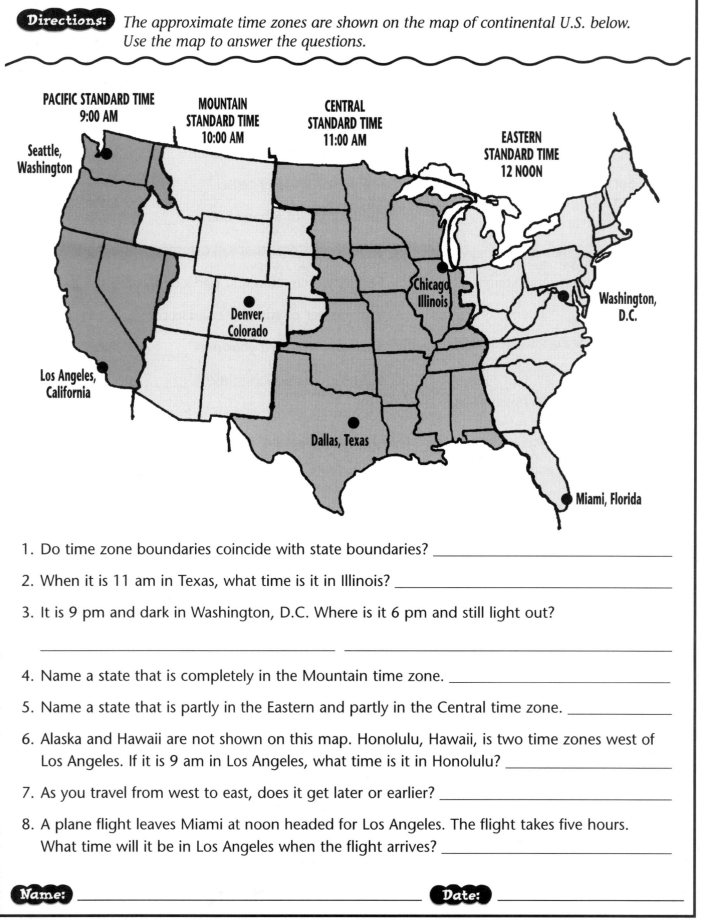

1. Do time zone boundaries coincide with state boundaries? _____

2. When it is 11 am in Texas, what time is it in Illinois? _____

3. It is 9 pm and dark in Washington, D.C. Where is it 6 pm and still light out?

   _____   _____

4. Name a state that is completely in the Mountain time zone. _____

5. Name a state that is partly in the Eastern and partly in the Central time zone. _____

6. Alaska and Hawaii are not shown on this map. Honolulu, Hawaii, is two time zones west of Los Angeles. If it is 9 am in Los Angeles, what time is it in Honolulu? _____

7. As you travel from west to east, does it get later or earlier? _____

8. A plane flight leaves Miami at noon headed for Los Angeles. The flight takes five hours. What time will it be in Los Angeles when the flight arrives? _____

Name: _____   **Date:** _____

Let me give it to you straight from the horse's mouth—an idiom is an expression that means something other than what the words really say. You dig?

Directions: *Each passage below contains an idiom. Underline it. Then imagine that you have to explain to a little kid what was really meant. Write your explanation on the lines.*

1. On her way home from school, Cassandra saw that someone had thrown trash on the sidewalk. "Littering drives me up the wall," she mumbled to herself.

_____

2. Jack tried out for the team, but when the results were posted his name did not appear on the list. It was a bitter pill to swallow.

_____

3. Melanie was studying for her science test. After an hour her head was swimming with facts. "I hope I remember all this," she thought as she turned out the light.

_____

4. Jeff's older brother Jim doesn't usually mind when Jeff wants to hang out in his room or play video games with him. But when Jim has friends over, that's a horse of a different color.

_____

5. At dinner, Mom asked Dad how his first day at his new job went. "It's all new to me," he said. "I obviously need some time to get my feet wet."

_____

6. Rachel had been looking forward all week to spending the weekend with her dad. When he called on Thursday night to say he couldn't make it, her heart sank.

_____

7. Brent answered the phone. It was for his brother, Andy. When Andy picked up the phone and found out it was Ellen, he suddenly got tongue-tied.

_____

Directions: Similes and metaphors are expressions used to make writing more colorful and interesting. First, study the meanings of these terms and the examples given. Next, identify each bold expression as a simile or metaphor. Finally, write its meaning.

Simile
An expression that compares one thing to another using like or as.
Examples: He ran like the wind.
It was as comfortable as an old shoe.

Metaphor
An expression that directly compares by substituting one thing for another.
Examples: They were busy beavers.
She had hair of gold.

1. Mom says **my room is a pig sty**.　O simile　O metaphor
_____

2. The **friends were two peas in a pod**.　O simile　O metaphor
_____

3. Arthur **sat like a bump on a log**.　O simile　O metaphor
_____

4. From age four, she **swam like a fish**.　O simile　O metaphor
_____

5. When I woke up, **my throat felt like sandpaper**.　O simile　O metaphor
_____

6. We entered the room **as quiet as mice**.　O simile　O metaphor
_____

7. Tonight I have **a mountain of homework**.　O simile　O metaphor
_____

8. **Pillows of cotton** drifted across the sky.　O simile　O metaphor
_____

Name: _____　**Date:** _____

Directions: *Read the passage and answer the questions.*

Nutty Trivia

For centuries hand ground peanuts were made into a paste and eaten by the Peruvian Indians and African tribes.

Ambrose Staub, a St. Louis doctor, invented a peanut mill in 1903 to make butter for elderly patients with weak teeth. Eventually, the idea caught on and these days peanut butter is a popular and nutritious staple in the American diet.

However, no one is quite certain who the first person was to combine peanut butter with jelly to make the now famous peanut butter and jelly sandwich.

1. **Who** invented the peanut mill.

   _____

2. **What** did the Peruvian Indians make ground peanuts into?

   _____

3. **Where** did Ambrose Staub practice medicine?

   _____

4. **When** was jelly added to peanut butter to make a sandwich?

   _____

   _____

5. **What** type of patients did Dr. Staub care for?_____

6. **Why** did Dr. Staub's patients need peanut butter? _____

   _____

7. **When** was the peanut mill invented?

   _____

Name: _____   **Date:** _____

Tracking Time

How was a year defined in Prehistoric times? No one knows for sure, but it is thought that people might have used monuments, such as Stonehenge in England, to track the sun's position in the sky in order to measure the length of a year.

The early Romans created a calendar based on the cycles of the moon. However, when Julius Caesar became Emperor of Rome around 45 B.C., he introduced the Julian calendar. This calendar marked time by measuring the Earth's revolution around the sun.

A few centuries later, Pope Gregory XIII appointed a team of learned men to help make the Julian calendar more accurate. It became known as the Gregorian calendar, and it is the system we still use today to chart the passage of a year.

1. **Who** introduced the Julian calendar?

    O Pope Gregory XIII   O Julius Caesar   O prehistoric people

2. **What** might monuments like Stonehenge have been used for?

    O to track the moon   O to track the Earth   O to track the sun

3. **Why** did Pope Gregory XIII appoint a team of men to revise the calendar?

    O He didn't like Caesar.   O no reason   O for accuracy

4. **When** did we stop using the Gregorian calendar?

    O in prehistoric times   O in 45 B.C.   O We still use it today.

5. **Where** is Stonehenge located?

    O in Rome   O in England   O in the U.S.A.

Name: _____   **Date:** _____

The Gettysburg Address

The Gettysburg Address is a very famous speech given by the 16th president of the United States, Abraham Lincoln. On November 19, 1863, he gave this speech in dedication of the Gettysburg National Cemetery in Pennsylvania, where countless Civil War soldiers lay buried.

President Lincoln was not the featured speaker for the event. He was only to say a few appropriate remarks after the featured orator, Edward Everett, gave what turned out to be a two-hour speech.

When it was his turn to address the assembled, President Lincoln rose to deliver the now-famous speech. It lasted less than three minutes, was only ten sentences long, and was received with only faint applause at the time. However, it became one of the more well-known orations in American history.

1. **Who:** _____

   A: Abraham Lincoln, the 16th president of the United States

2. **What:** _____

   A: The Gettysburg Address

3. **When:** _____

   A: November 19, 1863

4. **Why:** _____

   A: To dedicate the Gettysburg National Cemetery

5. **Where:** _____

   A: The cemetery was located in Gettysburg, Pennsylvania.

1. **Who** was King Thutmose I? _____

2. **What** does *pharaoh* mean? _____

3. **Where** is Hatshepsut shown wearing a beard? _____

4. **When** did Hatshepsut rule Egypt? _____

5. **Why** did she build her temple? _____

_____

Queen Hatshepsut, Pharaoh of Egypt

At the foot of tall cliffs on the west bank of the Nile river, near the Valley of the Kings in Egypt, stands a great temple. This temple was built in honor of Queen Hatshepsut who was the ruler of Egypt from 1512 to possibly 1482 B.C.

When her father, King Thutmose I, died, she and her brother ascended the throne. Shortly afterward, her brother died, leaving Hatshepsut to rule the land alone. Even though she was a woman, she had herself crowned as pharaoh, the Egyptian title meaning king or emperor. Ancient paintings show her wearing a false beard, a symbol for wisdom, only worn by pharaohs. She wore masculine clothing and the crown of the pharaoh, too.

Hatshepsut was a very able ruler and spent much of her reign concentrating on commercial enterprises and trades with other lands, as well as building beautiful temples and buildings. She built the temple on the Nile as a place for her body to rest when she died. She made sure it was an elaborate structure so that people would remember her as a pharaoh in her own right.

Name: _____

Date: _____

Eye is to see as ear is to hear. This kind of comparison is called an analogy. An analogy shows how things are related. (It's a skill commonly found on standardized tests!)

Directions: An analogy always has two pairs of words. The second pair of words must be related _in the same way_ as the first pair. Test your analogy skills below.

EXAMPLE:

broom is to _sweep_ as

cloth is to _____.

O _table_   O _wipe_   O _dirt_

The correct answer is wipe because sweep describes a broom's action, therefore wipe describes a cloth's action.

1. _hair_ is to _trim_ as

   grass is to _____.

   O _green_   O _grow_   O _mow_

2. _bear_ is to _den_ as

   bee is to _____.

   O _hive_   O _sting_   O _honey_

3. _illustrator_ is to _draw_ as

   author is to _____.

   O _write_   O _book_   O _read_

4. _orange_ is to _peel_ as

   egg is to _____.

   O _chicken_   O _yolk_   O _shell_

5. _woman_ is to _aunt_ as

   man is to _____.

   O _father_   O _uncle_   O _brother_

6. _cat_ is to _pet_ as

   red is to _____.

   O _rose_   O _blue_   O _color_

7. _dirt_ is to _mound_ as

   sand is to _____.

   O _castle_   O _dune_   O _beach_

8. _cars_ are to _roads_ as

   planes are to _____.

   O _sky_   O _fly_   O _jets_

9. _slither_ is to _snake_ as

   gallop is to _____.

   O _trot_   O _shed_   O _horse_

10. _clean_ is to _dirty_ as

    neat is to _____.

    O _closet_   O _clothes_   O _messy_

Name: _____   **Date:** _____

ACROSS

1. *eat* is to <u>hungry</u> as *drink* is to _____.

3. *bathroom* is to <u>tub</u> as *kitchen* is to _____.

5. *fish* is to <u>fin</u> as *seal* is to _____.

7. *hard* is to <u>rock</u> as *soft* is to _____.

10. *milk* is to <u>pudding</u> as *flour* is to _____.

11. *bottle* is to <u>cap</u> as *jar* is to _____.

12. *problem* is to <u>solution</u> as *question* is to _____.

DOWN

1. *cherry* is to <u>fruit</u> as *hammer* is to _____.

2. *false* is to <u>true</u> as *no* is to _____.

4. *keys* are to <u>piano</u> as *strings* are to _____.

5. *clap* is to <u>hands</u> as *run* is to _____.

6. *racquet* is to <u>tennis</u> as *stick* is to _____.

8. *rhinos* are to <u>horns</u> as *deer* are to _____.

9. *robin* is to <u>bird</u> as *dog* is to _____.

Name: _____   Date: _____

Directions: *Below is a list of stores and services available in a typical community. Answer each question with the best place to find what you are looking for.*

Community Service

veterinarian

department store

pharmacy

optometrist

party store

bakery

auto parts store

physician

gas station

office supply store

florist

pet supply store

1. Where could you find a special cake for a graduation party?

_____

2. Where could you get a doctor's prescription filled?

_____

3. Where could you take your puppy for a vaccination?

_____

4. Where could you shop for kitchen appliances?

_____

5. Where could you get a bouquet for Mother's Day?

_____

6. Where could you get a replacement carburetor?

_____

7. Where could you get an eye exam and be fitted for glasses?

_____

8. Where could you go to put air in your bicycle's tires?

_____

9. Where could you buy a cartridge for your printer?

_____

Name: _____   **Date:** _____

A	B	C	D	E-F	G	H	I-J	K-L	M	N	O	P	Q	R	S	T-U	V	W	X-Z
Vol. 1	Vol. 2	Vol. 3	Vol. 4	Vol. 5	Vol. 6	Vol. 7	Vol. 8	Vol. 9	Vol. 10	Vol. 11	Vol. 12	Vol. 13	Vol. 14	Vol. 15	Vol. 16	Vol. 17	Vol. 18	Vol. 19	Vol. 20

1. The inventions of Benjamin Franklin   Vol. _____ because

_____ .

2. Animals of the desert southwest   Vol. _____ because

_____ .

3. History of the Civil War   Vol. _____ because

_____ .

4. Rainforests of Brazil's Amazon Basin   Vol. _____ because

_____ .

5. The systems of the human body   Vol. _____ because

_____ .

6. Migration patterns of whales   Vol. _____ because

_____ .

Name: _____   Date: _____

What Doesn't Belong (Use the Clues)

1. shoelaces, ribbon, sequins, buttons, zipper, snaps

   Which does not belong with the rest? _____ *Why not?*

   _____

2. modern, ballroom, hula, tap, square, round, ballet, jazz

   Which does not belong with the rest? _____ *Why not?*

   _____

3. horse, whale, shark, bear, antelope, mouse, person, elephant

   Which does not belong with the rest? _____ *Why not?*

   _____

4. 3,705   4,702   609   42,803   2,645   75,206   504

   Which does not belong with the rest? _____ *Why not?*

   _____

5. maple, apple, oak, cactus, palm, lemon, willow

   Which does not belong with the rest? _____ *Why not?*

   _____

6. brown, blue, blonde, white, black, auburn, gray

   Which does not belong with the rest? _____ *Why not?*

   _____

7. kitten, adult, pup, kid, cub, cygnet, gosling

   Which does not belong with the rest? _____ *Why not?*

   _____

Name: _____   Date: _____

Each passage below is the beginning of a paragraph. Decide which purpose the author probably had in mind when he or she wrote it. Write one of the boldfaced words below.

All communication is done with a purpose in mind. A passage you read may have been written for one of these reasons:

- to **describe** something
- to **inform** or share knowledge
- to **summarize** or explain
- to **instruct** or give directions
- to **persuade** or convince
- to **entertain** or amuse

1. I don't know how or why, but I think I have the biggest cat in the world. His name is Rex but I'm thinking of changing it to T-Rex.

   _____

2. Year-round school, with its several short breaks throughout the year, is better than the traditional summer-off schedule.

   _____

3. Have you read *Miss Nelson Is Missing* by James Marshall? It is the hilarious story of a teacher with an unruly class, who teaches them to behave by disguising herself as a mean substitute named Miss Viola Swamp.

   _____

4. Making marshmallow rice treats can be fun, but messy. First you will need to gather all the ingredients.

   _____

5. On Saturday, May 28, our school will be having its annual field day. There will be lots of food, games, and field events in which children of all ages can participate.

   _____

6. I sat at the back of the rowboat and gazed at the orange glow of the warm sun as it set over the water that was lapping lazily at my feet.

   _____

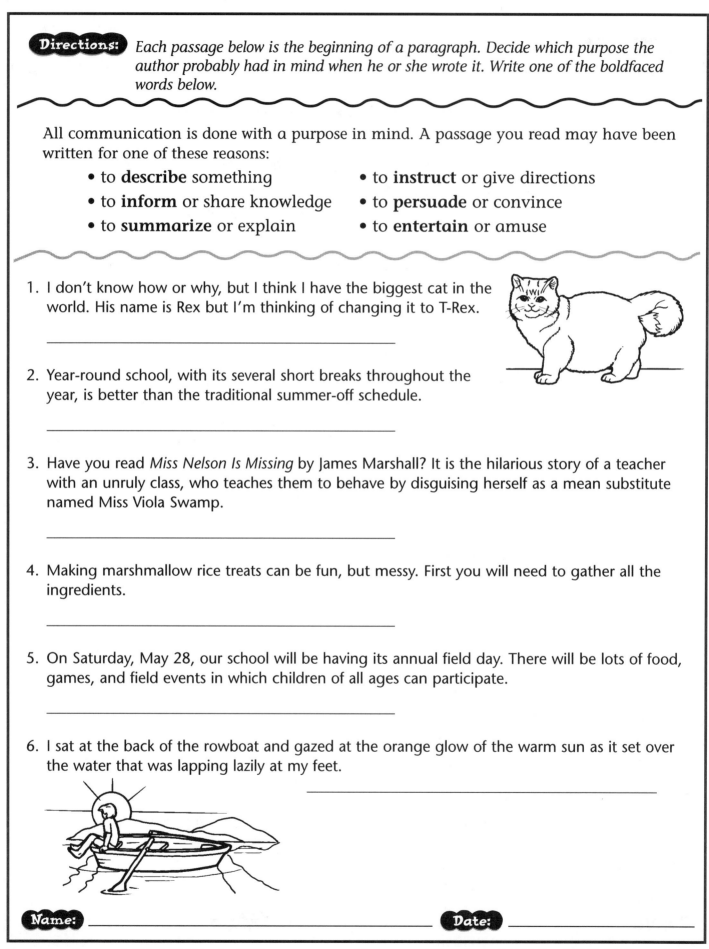

Name: _____   **Date:** _____

Directions: *Read each passage. Look for signals. Then, choose the correct time: past, present, or future.*

1. When dinosaurs ruled the land, the world looked very different from how it looks today. Where there are now dry plains, there were once fern-filled forests.

   The passage is about events in the

   O past
   O present
   O future

2. When we reached Saturn everyone was relieved. Our spaceship had had some technical difficulty as we navigated through the meteor shower.

   The passage is about events in the

   O past
   O present
   O future

3. I am a nutritionist at the city zoo. This year, I am teaching visiting groups about what it takes to feed a zoo population. I have to plan meals for approximately 7,000 animals each day.

   The passage is about events in the

   O past
   O present
   O future

4. Thousands stood up and cheered when the ball went into the net. Jose had scored the first winning goal in the 21st century.

   The passage is about events in the

   O past
   O present
   O future

5. My family and I live in North America. We are members of the Sioux tribe and live in a teepee.

   The passage is about events in the

   O past
   O present
   O future

6. Can you believe it? Grandpa told me that when he was a boy he did not have a computer, TV, cell phone, boom box, etc. Amazing!

   The passage is about events in the

   O past
   O present
   O future

Name: _____

Date: _____

What Next?/Then...

1. Mom rolled the shopping cart out of the grocery store and into the parking lot. Suddenly she realized she had forgotten where she parked. _____
   _____ .

2. Adam forgot that he was adding water to the pool. He went back outside and saw that the pool was overflowing. _____
   _____ .

3. Dad was on the riding mower. When he finished cutting the grass, he realized he did not have the garage door opener. _____
   _____ .

4. Pamela got ready for dance class and raced to the dance studio. When she got there the dance studio door was locked. _____
   _____ .

5. Michael and Sabrina were close friends. Then, Michael met Sara and starting hanging out exclusively with Sara. _____
   _____ .

6. Lori cooked an egg in the microwave. However, she programmed the microwave for 10 minutes! _____
   _____ .

Name: _____   **Date:** _____

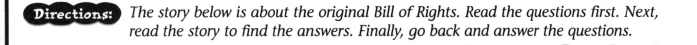

Do you read first and ask questions later? A better strategy is to ask questions before you read. Then read to find the answers.

Directions: *The story below is about the original Bill of Rights. Read the questions first. Next, read the story to find the answers. Finally, go back and answer the questions.*

1. What is the Bill of Rights? _____

2. Why was the Bill of Rights a priority for the new government? _____

   _____

   _____

3. How long did it take from the proposal to the ratification? _____

4. How many of the proposed amendments were finally accepted? _____

5. What was the main intent of the Bill of Rights? _____

   _____

6. How was the American version of the Bill of Rights different from the English version? _____

   _____

   _____

On April 30, 1789, the first president of the United States took office. For the newly independent country, a pressing order of business was to pass into law a set of amendments to the Constitution. This was important because several states had only agreed to adopting the Constitution if a specific Bill of Rights was added.

Led by Madison, a list of 12 amendments were proposed for ratification on September 25, 1789. Ten of the twelve were ratified and in force on December 15, 1791. These ten amendments are known as the Bill of Rights.

The main intent of the Bill of Rights was to guarantee freedoms not specifically addressed in the Constitution. Unlike similar provisions in the English version, in which Parliament could repeal a right, the American Bill of Rights could only be repealed through the states.

Name: _____ **Date:** _____

Formulating questions not only helps you focus on your purpose for reading, it can also improve your overall comprehension. Choose your favorite book. Then practice formulating questions about it. Write your questions on the lines.

1. Write three questions you would ask the main character (about the events of the story, his/her feelings at different times, his/her view of other characters, ...).

   Q. _____
   _____

   Q. _____
   _____

   Q. _____
   _____

2. Write three questions you would ask the supporting characters (about the events of the story, their feelings at different times, their view of other characters, ...).

   Q. _____
   _____

   Q. _____
   _____

   Q. _____
   _____

3. Write three questions you would ask the author, (about writing the story, his/her views of characters or events, where he/she got his/her ideas, ...).

   Q. _____
   _____

   Q. _____
   _____

   Q. _____
   _____

Name: _____ **Date:** _____

Directions: *Read the statements and answer the questions.*

1. Dad said cleaning the garage would take "a month of Sundays."

   How long would that really be? _____

2. In 2001, Leslie celebrated her eleventh birthday.

   In what year was Leslie born? _____

3. With the signing of the Declaration of Independence in 1776, the country of the United States was formed.

   About how old is the nation? _____

4. Mom got a notice announcing her 20th high school reunion.

   When did Mom graduate from high school? _____

5. There was work to be done. The crops were ready to harvest.

   What time of year is it? _____

6. Grandpa was 27 when Dad was born, Dad was 27 when I was born, and I am 10.

   How old is Grandpa? _____

7. The music was composed in the mid-19th century.

   About what year was it? _____

8. Sam drove two hours on the freeway, averaging about 60 mph.

   About how many miles did he cover? _____

Name: _____   **Date:** _____

A Visit to the Commissary

One warm day in late May, 43 students, two teachers, and six parents boarded the school bus for a trip to the National Zoo in Washington, D.C. In less than an hour they arrived. The group had been studying nutrition and were about to learn what it takes to feed a zoo.

The zoo nutritionist was waiting for them when they arrived. Before they went to see any animals, they got to take a peek at the area where food is ordered, received, and sorted. The nutritionist pointed out that feeding about 7,000 animals is quite a feat. "You'd be amazed," she said. "For example, a single gray seal eats about 25 pounds of fish a day. Four big cats consume more than 450 pounds of meat each week. And, believe it or not, we order crickets from a cricket farm—some 38,000 at a time."

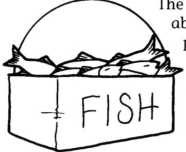

The children were amazed as the nutritionist told them even more about the menu of incredible proportions.

Later, as the children walked around and observed the animals, they saw them in a different light. In fact, they would never think of the zoo again without imagining the tons of food it takes to feed its residents.

1. What best describes a commissary?

   O a storage area   O a kitchen   O an area set aside for animals

2. Was the zoo nutritionist a man or a woman?

   O man   O woman   O story doesn't say

3. The school was within driving distance of Washington, D.C.

   O true   O false   O can't tell

4. Why was the nutritionist waiting for them?

   O The nutritionist greets everyone.   O The meeting was prearranged.

5. For what animals does the zoo need to order crickets?

   O lions & tigers   O gray seals   O story doesn't say

6. What does "in a different light" mean?

   O brighter   O in a new way   O stranger than before

Name: _____   **Date:** _____

The Olmec

When archaeologists slashed through the jungles of Central America, they uncovered one of the oldest and most baffling civilizations on the continent—the Olmec.

Around 1200 B.C. this advanced culture was able to clear incredibly dense jungle to raise crops. Bountiful harvests supplied a surplus of food, which enabled some of the people to devote their attention to other matters. The Olmec constructed cities, formed a government, and became skilled artists and sculptors. They developed a calendar, a counting system, and a form of hieroglyphic writing—all of which would influence the later civilizations of the region.

The Olmec culture thrived for about 1,000 years, yet much of who they were and how they lived is still shrouded in mystery.

1. Are the jungles of Central America thin or thick? _____

   Which word tells you so? _____

2. Do we fully understand the Olmec civilization? _____

   Which word tells you so? _____

3. Did the Olmec have plenty or not enough food? _____

   Which word tells you so? _____

4. Was the Olmec writing in letters or pictures? _____

   Which word tells you so? _____

5. Did the Olmec have an effect on future cultures? _____

   Which word tells you so? _____

6. Do we know much or little about the Olmec? _____

   Which word tells you so? _____

Name: _____   Date: _____

Directions: *An expression (or idiom) is a phrase that means something other than what the words say. Use the clues in each passage below to figure out and describe each person below. Then write the meaning of the bold phrase.*

1. When Ms. Jones called on Sue to answer, she didn't know because her **head was in the clouds.**

_____

2. Suddenly, **out of the blue**, the correct answer popped into Sandra's head.

_____

3. The fact that Grandma, Mom, and I are all good at art proves that **the fruit doesn't fall far from the tree**.

_____

4. Mario's responsible behavior and attitude show that he has his **feet planted firmly in the ground**.

_____

5. Don't bother waiting for Abby to call you back—it could be a **month of Sundays.**

_____

6. Kelly tried to explain why she had missed the last three meetings, but her story was **full of holes**.

_____

7. Leo was **walking on air** when he heard that he had won a ribbon in the science fair.

_____

8. It didn't make a **hill of beans difference** to Britt that she had never ridden a horse before. She was willing to try.

_____

Reading Comprehension • Saddleback Publishing, Inc. ©2002   50   3 Watson, Irvine, CA 92618•Phone (888)SDL-BACK• www.sdlback.com

Directions: *Read the passage. Then, answer the questions.*

The Snowy Owl

Among North American birds, the snowy owl ranks first in size. It can reach 27 inches in length and have a wingspan of 5 feet. The snowy owl is light for its size— about four pounds. It is easily distinguished from other large owls within its habitat by its predominately white plumage. The adult has few natural enemies, but eggs and juveniles are in danger from Arctic foxes and husky dogs.

Owls depend on their keen sense of hearing and the efficiency of their sight, which is designed to work well in the dark. Unlike most other owls that primarily hunt at night, the snowy owl is diurnal, making it well-suited to survive in the far north where it can be continuously light or dark around the clock. These owls mainly feed on lemmings, voles, and rabbits but are known to eat other birds and fish as well. The snowy owl can fly long distances carrying an animal weighing far more than itself.

1. Where is the snowy owl's habitat? _____

   How can you tell?_____

2. What color plumage do other owls of the region have?_____

   How can you tell? _____

3. Does the snowy owl hunt during the day, at night, or both? _____

   What word tells you? _____

4. Is the snowy owl a carnivore or herbivore? _____

   How can you tell? _____

5. Could the snowy owl carry off a rabbit weighing five pounds? _____

   How do you know? _____

Name: _____   **Date:** _____

How Do You Feel?

ACROSS

5. You are about to get a tooth pulled. You are ____.
7. You just won an award. You are____.
8. You stepped on a worm. You are ____.
10. Your friend told a lie about you. You are____.
11. Your mom is late picking you up. You are___.
12. You stayed up late studying. You are ___.

DOWN

1. You know you can do something well. You are _____.
2. You have nothing to do. You are_____.
3. You are motivated to do something. You are _____.
4. You don't understand how to do something. You are____.
6. You don't have to do something you dreaded. You are___.
9. You make a solemn promise. You are ___.

Word Box
relieved
inspired
mad
delighted
confident
concerned
disgusted
serious
bored
confused
nervous
exhausted

Name: _____ Date: _____

Pueblo Village

The Pueblo lived in what is now Arizona and New Mexico long before the Spanish arrived. Their homes are made of adobe, a sun-dried brick. Sometimes many dwellings were built together, side-by-side and stacked, housing hundreds of people.

When you look at pictures of a Pueblo village, does something strike you as odd? These Native Americans built their dwellings without doors—at least the type usually seen—an entrance at ground level. The "door" to a Pueblo home is typically an opening in the roof. Wooden ladders were used to scale the buildings.

1. The word Pueblo is used as a noun and an adjective. What does the noun mean?

   _____

2. Explain the meaning of each of these words as used in the story:

   strike: _____

   scale: _____

3. Adobe was defined as "sun-dried brick." What do you think these bricks are made of?

   _____

4. For what reason do you think the Pueblo put their "doors" on the roof?

   _____

5. What do you think was done with the ladders when all were inside?

   _____

1. It is a wooden or metal structure with padding on top. It is used to help support you as you walk if you have an injured leg or foot.

2. It is a special kind of hat. It may be made of silver or gold with other gems as decoration. It is worn by royalty.

3. It is a machine that picks up waves through the air and turns them into sounds. You can tune it to pick up the sound source you want.

4. It is a container for holding water or other liquids to drink. It is usually made of metal or plastic enclosed in a cloth cover. It has a strap for carrying it along with you.

5. It is a piece of cloth worn over the clothing to protect them from dirt or spills. It may be worn by a cook or other person who works with potentially messy materials.

6. It is a hand-held machine with buttons that show numbers and mathematical symbols. It is used to add, subtract, and perform other operations with numbers.

Name: _____ **Date:** _____

Good readers get a jump on what they are about to read by previewing and predicting Table of Contents, headings, and captions. Give it a try!

Directions: *A table of contents can help you preview and predict what the book is about. Use the table of contents below to answer the questions.*

Table of Contents

1. In what chapter would you find information about inland explorers? _____

2. What pages offer information about Columbus' voyages? _____

3. Do these chapters cover exploration prior to 1500? _____

4. The Cape of Good Hope is at the southern tip of Africa. Who sailed around it? _____

5. Balboa discovered the Pacific Ocean. Was this before or after John Cabot's time? _____

6. Magellan *circumnavigated* the world. What does that mean? _____

7. According to this book, what constitutes "early" exploration? _____

8. These chapters do not mention polar exploration. Why do you think that is so? _____

_____

9. What type of book is this table of contents likely to be from? _____

Name: _____   **Date:** _____

The Nile Crocodile is the largest reptile in Africa

Physical Characteristics

xxxxxx xxxxxxx xxxxx xxxx xxxxx xxxxxxxx xxxxxx xxxxx xxx xxxxxx xxxx xxx xxxxxx, xxxxxxx xxxxxxxx x xxxxxxxxxxx. xxxxxxxxx xxx x xxxx xxxx xxxx xxxx, xxxxx x xxxx xxx xxxxxxx, xxxxxx xx xxxxxx xxxx.
xxxxxx xxxxxxx xxxxx xxxx xxxxx xxxxxxxx xxxxxx xxxxx xxx xxxxxx xxxx xxx xxxxxx, xxxxxxx xxxxxxxx x xxxxxxxxxxx. xxxxxxxxx xxx x xxxx xxxx xxxx xxxx, xxxxx x xxxx xxx xxxxxxx, xxxxxx xx xxxxxx xxxx. xxxxxx xxxxxxx xxxxx xxxx xxxxx xxxxxxxx xxxxxx xxxxx xxx xxxxxx xxxx xxx xxxxxx, xxxxxxx xxxxxxxx x xxxxxxxxxxx, xxxxxxxxx xxx x xxxx xxxx xxxx xxxxx. xxxxx x xxxx xxx xxxxxxx, xxxxxx xx xxxxxx xxxx.

Habitat

xxxxxx xxxxxxx xxxxx xxxx xxxxx xxxxxxxx xxxxxx xxxxx xxx xxxxxx xxxx xxx xxxxxx, xxxxxxx xxxxxxxx x xxxxxxxxxxx. xxxxxxxxx xxx x xxxx xxxx xxxx xxxx, xxxxx x xxxx xxx xxxxxxx, xxxxxx xx xxxxxx xxxx.
xxxxxx xxxxxxx xxxxx xxxx xxxxx xxxxxxxx xxxxxx xxxxx xxx xxxxxx xxxx xxx xxxxxx, xxxxxxx xxxxxxxx x xxxxxxxxxxx. xxxxxxxxx xxx x xxxx xxxx xxxx xxxx, xxxxx x xxxx xxx xxxxxxx, xxxxxx xx xxxxxx xxxx. xxxxxx xxxxxxx xxxxx xxxx xxxxx xxxxxxxx xxxxxx xxxxx xxx xxxxxx xxxx xxx xxxxxx, xxxxxxx xxxxxxxx x xxxxxxxxxxx, xxxxxxxxx xxx x xxxx xxxx xxxx xxxxx. xxxxx x xxxx xxx xxxxxxx, xxxxxx xx xxxxxx xxxx.

Behavior—A Fearsome Carnivore

xxxxxx xxxxxxx xxxxx xxxx xxxxx xxxxxxxx xxxxxx xxxxx xxx xxxxxx xxxx xxx xxxxxx, xxxxxxx xxxxxxxx x xxxxxxxxxxx. xxxxxxxxx xxx x xxxx xxxx xxxx xxxx, xxxxx x xxxx xxx xxxxxxx, xxxxxx xx xxxxxx xxxx.
xxxxxx xxxxxxx xxxxx xxxx xxxxx xxxxxxxx xxxxxx xxxxx xxx xxxxxx xxxx xxx xxxxxx, xxxxxxx xxxxxxxx x xxxxxxxxxxx. xxxxxxxxx xxx x xxxx xxxx xxxx xxxx, xxxxx x xxxx xxx xxxxxxx, xxxxxx xx xxxxxx xxxx. xxxxxx xxxxxxx xxxxx xxxx xxxxx xxxxxxxx xxxxxx xxxxx xxx xxxxxx xxxx xxx xxxxxx, xxxxxxx xxxxxxxx x xxxxxxxxxxx, xxxxxxxxx xxx x xxxx xxxx xxxx xxxxx. xxxxx x xxxx xxx xxxxxxx, xxxxxx xx xxxxxx xxxx.

The Human Factor

xxxxxx xxxxxxx xxxxx xxxx xxxxx xxxxxxxx xxxxxx xxxxx xxx xxxxxx xxxx xxx xxxxxx, xxxxxxx xxxxxxxx x xxxxxxxxxxx. xxxxxxxxx xxx x xxxx xxxx xxxx xxxx, xxxxx x xxxx xxx xxxxxxx, xxxxxx xx xxxxxx xxxx.
xxxxxx xxxxxxx xxxxx xxxx xxxxx xxxxxxxx xxxxxx xxxxx xxx xxxxxx xxxx xxx xxxxxx, xxxxxxx xxxxxxxx x xxxxxxxxxxx. xxxxxxxxx xxx x xxxx xxxx xxxx xxxx, xxxxx x xxxx xxx xxxxxxx, xxxxxx xx xxxxxx xxxx. xxxxxx xxxxxxx xxxxx xxxx xxxxx xxxxxxxx xxxxxx xxxxx xxx xxxxxx xxxx xxx xxxxxx, xxxxxxx xxxxxxxx x xxxxxxxxxxx. xxxxxxxxx xxx x xxxx xxxx xxxx xxxx, xxxxx x xxxx xxx xxxxxxx, xxxxxx xx xxxxxx xxxx.

Related Species

xxxxxx xxxxxxx xxxxx xxxx xxxxx xxxxxxxx xxxxxx xxxxx xxx xxxxxx xxxx xxx xxxxxx, xxxxxxx xxxxxxxx x xxxxxxxxxxx. xxxxxxxxx xxx x xxxx xxxx xxxx xxxx, xxxxx x xxxx xxx xxxxxxx, xxxxxx xx xxxxxx xxxx.
xxxxxx xxxxxxx xxxxx xxxx xxxxx xxxxxxxx xxxxxx xxxxx xxx xxxxxx xxxx xxx xxxxxx, xxxxxxx xxxxxxxx x xxxxxxxxxxx. xxxxxxxxx xxx x xxxx xxxx xxxx xxxx, xxxxx x xxxx xxx xxxxxxx, xxxxxx xx xxxxxx xxxx.x

A noticeable difference is the teeth

Nile Crocodile

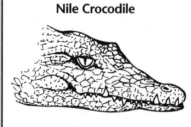

American Alligator

1. What is the subject of the page?

_____

2. What is one way you can tell a crocodile from an alligator?

_____

3. On what continent is the Nile River?

_____

4. What does a crocodile eat?

_____

5. What type of animal is a crocodile?

_____

6. Will this page give a description of a Nile crocodile's size?

_____

7. Will this page tell you about the habits of the American alligator?

_____

8. Do Nile crocodiles ever encounter humans?

_____

9. Will this page tell you what other animals are similar to the crocodile?

 Name: _____   **Date:** _____

Directions: Pictures, tables, graphs, and other visual graphics used to help illustrate text can be a very valuable aid in previewing and predicting what you are going to read. Imagine that this graphic appeared with an article on rivers. Answer the questions about what you can determine just from the picture.

Each line represents 100 miles in length

1,000   2,000   3,000   4,000

AMAZON (South America)

CONGO (Africa)

VOLGA (Europe)

NILE (Egypt)

MISSISSIPPI (U.S.)

COLORADO (U.S.)

1. Is this a picture, table, or graph? _____

2. Of the rivers shown, which is the shortest? _____

3. What river is greater than 2,500 miles long but less than 3,000 miles? _____

4. Is the Mississippi longer or shorter than the Colorado? _____

5. What is the only European river mentioned? _____

6. What two rivers are only a few hundred feet different in length?

_____

7. The U.S. is about 3,000 miles across. What two rivers are longer than the U.S. is wide?

_____

*Predict what the accompanying article will likely cover or not cover. Write **yes** or **no** next to each:*

8. _____ The article will compare lengths of the world's longest rivers.

9. _____ The article will talk about the rivers' direction of flow (north-south; east-west).

10. _____ The article will talk about other rivers, such as the Missouri.

11. _____ The article will talk only about rivers in the United States.

12. _____ The article will give the location and description of the rivers shown.

Name: _____   Date: _____

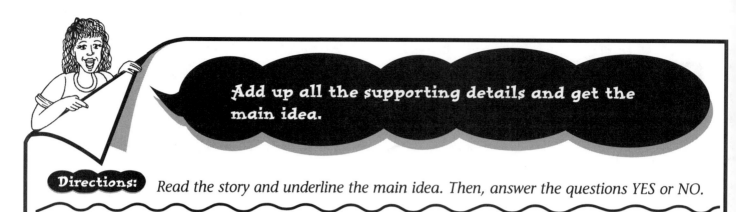

Directions: *Read the story and underline the main idea. Then, answer the questions YES or NO.*

Samuel F. B. Morse

Samuel F. B. Morse is instantly recognized as the inventor of Morse Code—a widely used system of dots and dashes transmitted over wire. His device, the telegraph, eventually made him wealthy and famous.

Though Morse is considered a successful inventor, his success was preceded by some very lean years.

Morse began not as an inventor but as a painter. Although recognized as talented, he did not make much money at his craft. While on a ship homeward bound from Europe, the almost penniless Morse became fascinated with the idea of sending messages across wires.

He took a job as an art teacher and used the little money he made to work on his idea. In 1844, after 12 years of work, he finally succeeded in impressing the world with his invention.

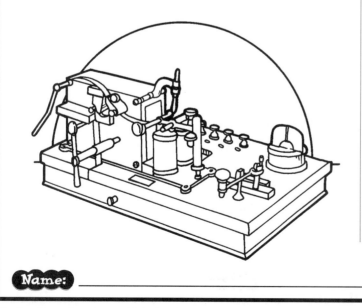

1. Was Morse Code named after its inventor?

   _____

2. Did Samuel Morse come from a wealthy background?

   _____

3. Did Morse grow up knowing he wanted to be an inventor?

   _____

4. Was Morse a recognized painter before he invented the telegraph?

   _____

5. Did Morse ever earn much money from his invention?

   _____

6. Did Morse get his idea for the telegraph while on a ship to Europe?

   _____

7. Did Morse spend over a decade working on his invention?

   _____

8. Is Samuel Morse still alive today?

   _____

Name: _____ **Date:** _____

Your teeth may be part of your smile, but they have a more important job—they are the first step in the process of digestion.

You have three kinds of teeth. In the very front of your mouth are eight flat, thin teeth called incisors. They are used for cutting and biting food. Next to these are pointed teeth called canines, which also help you tear food. The remaining teeth are molars. These teeth have flat tops for crushing and grinding the food.

1. What is the most important function of your teeth? _____

_____

2. What are the three kinds of teeth?_____

_____

3. How do your front teeth differ from your back teeth? _____

_____

If you take a close look at your tongue you will see that it is covered with tiny bumps called taste buds. They contain nerves that send messages to your brain that give you the sense of taste.

Your tongue can only detect four kinds of tastes—sweet, sour, salty, and bitter. The taste buds that pick up these signals are arranged on your tongue in different places. Look at the diagram to see where you would most strongly sense each taste.

bitter

sour   sour

salty   salty

sweet

4. What gives you the sensation of taste? _____

5. What are the only four tastes your tongue can detect? _____

_____

6. Why do you think people like to lick ice-cream with the tip of their tongue?

_____

(A)

_____ 1. On most days, you can easily see the star nearest Earth because it is our sun.

_____ 2. It does not look like other stars because it is so close relative to the other stars.

_____ 3. Still, it is quite a distance away—about 93 million miles from Earth!

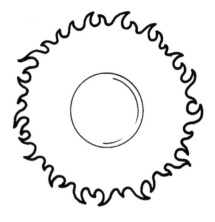

(B)

_____ 1. Sometimes a writer does not use his or her real name as an author.

_____ 2. One of the most famous pen names is Dr. Seuss, whose real name was Theodor Geisel.

_____ 3. When an author uses a made-up name for writing, it is called a pen name.

(C)

_____ 1. They are highly nutritious and their sweet taste makes them an excellent snack.

_____ 2. Raisins are dried grapes.

_____ 3. Though once considered a delicacy, raisins are readily available for snacking and cooking.

(D)

_____ 1. Some slugs have a small, flat shell under the skin, but most have no shell at all.

_____ 2. Like other snails, slugs have slimy skin that allows them to move about and protects their delicate bodies.

_____ 3. A slug is a kind of snail.

Name: _____   **Date:** _____

(A)

Latin is an ancient language that still lives today. Many English words are derived from Latin roots. For example, the Latin root *port* means "carry." So, *portable* means able to be carried; *transport* means carry across, *export* means carry out; *import* means carry in. In fact, *trans*, *ex*, and *im* are also Latin for "across," "out," and "in." Some English words also come from other languages, such as Greek.

1. Underline the sentence that gives the main idea.

2. Cross out the sentence that gives a detail that does not belong.

3. Write a good title: _____

(B) Ceramics is the shaping and heating of materials to create useful or beautiful objects. It is one of the most ancient arts. Native American pottery is among the most beautiful. Most ancient ceramics were made from clay, which was baked to harden, then painted or carved with designs. Pottery made by people thousands of years ago has been found intact. Today, ceramic pieces are also made from various other materials and for a wide range of uses from art objects to dental work.

1. Underline the sentence that gives the main idea.

2. Cross out the sentence that gives a detail that does not belong.

3. Write a good title: _____

Name: _____   **Date:** _____

Reading Comprehension • Saddleback Publishing, Inc. ©2002   61   3 Watson, Irvine, CA 92618•Phone (888)SDL-BACK• www.sdlback.com

Mount St. Helens

May 18, 1980, started out like many other days at the lodge at the foothills of Mount St. Helens—clear and calm. Some folks had lived the last fifty years on the shores of Spirit Lake in this beautiful area of Washington state. But this day was to change the face of the land to something unrecognizable.

There had been warnings of a possible eruption and many people had left the area. At 8:32 am an earthquake triggered a landslide on the sleeping giant. Gases and magma trapped in the mountain suddenly had an escape route! In barely a blink of an eye, Mount St. Helens exploded with the force of 500 atomic bombs. A huge cloud of super hot gases, rock, steam, and ash spewed out, disintegrating the top of the mountain and surrounding area. Then a moving wall of debris came down the mountain, wiping out everything in its path. The lake was emptied. And the lodge? Buried under 40 feet of ash and mud. The blast zone covered an area of more than 230 square miles, leaving vast stretches of leveled trees and barren land.

1. Where is Mount St. Helens located?

   O Washington, D.C.   O Canada   O Washington state

2. What finally triggered the blast?

   O earthquake   O landslide   O atomic bomb

3. To what does "sleeping giant" refer?

   O Spirit Lake   O volcano   O the lodge

4. Until this time, Mount St. Helens had not erupted since 1857. How long had it been since it last erupted?

   O 133 years   O 177 years   O 123 years

5. Why had many people left the area before the eruption?

   O They felt an earthquake.   O They'd been warned.   O They heard the explosion.

Name: _____   **Date:** _____

The Boy Who Cried Wolf

A shepherd boy was in charge of tending his master's sheep near a dark forest not far from the village. But being a boy, he found the task dull and lonely. He wondered what he could do to relieve his boredom. Remembering that his master instructed him to call for help if a wolf should appear, he decided to call "Wolf" though none was there.

Immediately the villagers came rushing to his aid. But when they arrived, they found no threat. The boy was amused by this, so the next week he did the same thing. Again the villagers came and again found no wolf.

The next week it came to pass that a wolf did come out of the woods and threaten the sheep. The boy cried, "Wolf! Wolf" but the villagers did not come. They were determined not to be fooled again.

1. What is the main idea of this fable? _____
   _____

2. Why did the boy cry 'Wolf"

   the first time? _____

   the second time?_____

   the third time?_____

3. Why did the villagers not come to the boy's rescue the third time?

   O They didn't hear him.   O They didn't believe him.

4. Find the word in the story that means:

   help: _____   boring: _____

   caring for: _____   entertained: _____

   woods: _____   hurrying: _____

5. A fable is a story that has a moral, or lesson to be learned, such as, *Actions speak louder than words* or *Some things are easier said than done*. Write what you think the moral of this story is:

   _____
   _____

Imagine your family is planning a two-day trip. Below is the information you got when you requested a travel package from the Blue Hills Inn. Read the offer carefully. Then answer the questions below.

Special Offer—Limited Time Only!

If you have a family of four and want a two-day outing filled with fun, take advantage of our "4-2-3" special (four guests, two nights, $300). The special also includes four tickets for the Blue Hills jeep tour (a $60 value) and a $40 credit toward dinner at the Blue Hills Restaurant.

While in the Blue Hills, your family will want to visit the aquarium in nearby Springsville, so we are also throwing in four passes for the shuttle bus—an additional savings of $12.

If this sounds like something your family would enjoy, you'd better hurry. Our "4-2-3" special is good only from Feb. 1-June 1. Call today for reservations! 1-800-000-0000

1. What does the "2" stand for in the "4-2-3" special?

    O 2 nights   O 2 guests   O 2 hundred dollars

2. How much is a single ticket for the jeep tour?

    O $60   O $15   O $12

3. For how long a period is Blue Hills offering this special?

    O 5 months   O 30 days   O 4 months

4. For a family of four, what is the cost of this package per person?

    O $75   O $90   O $112   O $37.50

5. Why would this offer not be a good choice for

    a) a family of 3? _____

    b) a family with a baby? _____

6. What is the main benefit of this offer?_____

    _____

Rattlers

Rattlesnakes are among the most feared of reptiles. This fear is well-deserved because, though most snakes are harmless, rattlers are poisonous. Some are large and some are small, but all have the characteristic segments at the end of their tails, which they shake to produce the rattle sound.

Rattlers range in size from under two feet to seven or more feet in length. The diamondback rattler, easily recognized by the diamond-shaped markings along its back, is the most bulky of all poisonous snakes, though not the longest. Other smaller rattlers include the pygmy rattlesnake and the timber rattler.

It is believed by some that the age of a rattlesnake corresponds to the number of segments of its rattle. But, actually a rattler adds a segment each time it sheds its skin—up to four times a year. And, when about ten segments accumulate, they start to fall off.

1. The pygmy rattler is among the smaller of the rattlesnake varieties.

_____

2. The timber rattler is a poisonous snake.

_____

3. Rattlesnakes eat birds and small mammals.

_____

4. A rattlesnake does not always rattle before striking.

_____

5. There are more kinds of harmless snakes than poisonous ones.

_____

6. A rattlesnake adds one rattle segment per year.

_____

7. The diamondback rattler is the heaviest of all poisonous snakes.

_____

8. Other poisonous snakes include the cobra and coral snake.

_____

Name: _____   **Date:** _____

An outline is like a skeleton—a basic framework on which to build the "meat" of a story or passage.

Directions: *Imagine it is the first day of school. Your teacher has passed out the outline below to study, then, use it to introduce yourself to the group. Write what you would say.*

Main topics are listed as Roman Numerals.

Subtopics are indented and listed with capital letters, followed by a period.

If a subtopic has separate key points, they are indented further and listed by number.

Each line begins with a capital letter.

I. **Who I am**
   A. **Description**
   B. **Family**

II. **What I like**
   A. **Favorite subject**
   B. **Hobbies/Interests**

III. **My Plans**
   A. **This school year**
   B. **When I'm grown**
     1. **Where I'll live**
     2. **What I'll do**

_____
_____
_____
_____
_____
_____
_____
_____
_____
_____
_____
_____
_____
_____
_____
_____

Name: _____ **Date:** _____

An outline provides the "bare bones" of information. Read and follow the directions below to create an outline of how the U.S. government is structured.

The U.S. constitution divides the powers of American government into three branches, each with its own powers and limitations.

Study the basic outline framework below. Then use it to help you fill in the missing parts on the outline at the right.

I. (Branch)
   A. (Who)
   B. (Main purpose)
   C. (Main powers)
     1. (Power)
     2. (Power)
     3. (Power)

- Represent general population
- Supreme Court
- Command armed forces
- Main powers of Judicial Branch
- President
- Impeach the President
- Declare laws unconstitutional
- Set foreign policy
- Declare war
- Veto laws from Congress
- Legislative Branch

Structure of the U.S. Government

I. Executive Branch
   A. _____
   B. Oversees and administers government
   C. Main powers of Executive Branch
     1. _____
     2. Appoint high federal officials
     3. _____
     4. _____

II. _____
   A. House of Representatives and Senate (Congress)
   B. _____
   C. Main powers of Legislative Branch
     1. Propose new laws
     2. _____
     3. Levy taxes and appropriate funds
     4. _____

III. Judicial Branch
   A. _____
   B. Judges constitutionality of laws
   C. _____
     1. Uphold existing laws
     2. _____
     3. Settle legal disputes from lower courts

Directions: *Practice summarizing. Imagine you will be tested on the information in each passage below. Take notes of the key points you want to remember. Then write a brief summary.*

A. The "Cold War" was one in which no shots were fired. The term refers to the cooling, then fiercely opposing ideology differences that developed between the U.S. and primarily Russia in the years following World War II. The "war" was one of competition in politics, economics, and propaganda. Neither side trusted the other and both sides were convinced that only their own would prevail. The space race epitomized this period of time.

Key point: What was the "Cold War"? _____

Key point: Who were the main adversaries? _____

Key point: What kind of "war" was waged? _____

Summary: _____

_____

B. In 1803, the size of the United States doubled under President Jefferson. A vast amount of land, some 828,000 square miles, had been held by Spain but recently ceded to France. The territory extended from the Gulf coast to the current Canadian border extending out from the Mississippi basin. Napoleon, unable to gain a strong foothold in the New World, decided that rather than fight to retain this territory (and most likely lose it), he would sell it to the United States for about 15 million dollars. The Louisiana Purchase was one of President Jefferson's grandest achievements.

Key point: How did the U.S. double in size in 1803? _____

Key point: Who sold and purchased the land? _____

_____

Key point: What was the location and size of the territory? _____

_____

Summary: _____

_____

The Greedy Brother

A thousand years ago there lived two Chinese brothers. One was very wealthy but miserly. The other was poor but generous. The wealthy brother, whose name was Kim, spent all of his time figuring out how to increase his wealth. The poor brother, whose name was Cho, shared with his neighbors what little he had.

By and by came a time when it rained for many days. The rice in Cho's little paddy would not grow, for it was at the bottom of the hill. Kim, who raised silkworms, was not affected. Cho climbed the hill to ask his brother for help.

Kim had many silkworms, whose thread he sold at a large profit. Kim did not want to give his brother anything valuable, but only to appear to be helping him. Kim gave Cho a box of worms that he thought were near dead. Cho thanked him and took them home.

Cho fed the worms generously with mulberry leaves and they grew fat and healthy. Soon Cho had silk to sell. When Kim heard of this, he became enraged at his brother's good fortune. One night he sneaked down the hill and cut all Cho's worms in half.

Instead of dying, each of Cho's worms regenerated, so he had twice as many as before. Upon hearing this, Kim became more enraged. He went out into his own collection and cut all his own worms in half. But, Kim's worms died and he lost his fortune.

Cho never knew what his brother had done or why. He just took him into his modest home and cared for Kim for the rest of his life.

Who? _____

What? _____

_____

Where? _____ When? _____

Why? _____

_____

Summary: _____

_____

_____

_____

_____

_____

Name: _____ Date: _____

Reading is like detective work. You must be able to distinguish facts from opinions and specifics from generalizations. Test your reading detective skills.

Directions: Each sentence below is either a fact or an opinion AND a specific detail or a generalization. Mark each as follows: Specific Fact, Specific Opinion, General Fact, or General Opinion.

Specific Fact
The brown bat is common in the United States.

General Fact
Insect-eating bats use echo-location to find food.

Specific Opinion
Vampire bats are the scariest bat.

General Opinion
Bats are ugly and creepy.

_____ 1. Like dogs, mice, and cats, all bats are mammals.

_____ 2. Bats have odd-looking faces and heads.

_____ 3. There are several hundred species of bats worldwide.

_____ 4. Little brown bats make excellent pets.

_____ 5. Bats sleep hanging upside down.

_____ 6. Bats are helpful to us because they eat vast numbers of insects.

_____ 7. People should be afraid of and avoid bats.

_____ 8. Bats are the only mammals that can fly.

_____ 9. The flying fox is a bat found in Southeast Asia.

_____ 10. Bats are nocturnal—they are most active at night.

_____ 11. Unlike most bats, flying foxes eat fruit.

_____ 12. The snout of a horseshoe bat looks like a smashed leaf.

Name: _____   **Date:** _____

Directions: *A generalization is a statement that can be concluded about a group of specifics. To be valid, a generalization must be true for all things and in all cases. Read each description. Choose the sentence that states a valid generalization.*

A. Sara lives in Arizona. The summers are long and very hot, but Sara loves it because she enjoys swimming and can go for all but a couple of months a year. Josh lives in Wisconsin, where the winters are cold and snowy. He loves going sledding and ice-skating. Abby lives in Pennsylvania. Her favorite thing about living there is the change of seasons.

O It is better to live in a place with seasons.

O There is no place to live where you can both swim and sled.

O People enjoy living in different types of climates.

B. Green plants contain chlorophyll, which enables them to make their own food. They require sunlight, water, minerals, and carbon dioxide to do this. Other plants, such as molds, mushrooms, and yeasts, depend on food from other sources. Mold grows and feeds on such things as bread and fruit. Mushrooms get their food from soil or decaying wood. Yeasts can live on the sugar in water.

O True plants make their own food.

O Some plants make their own food; others do not.

O Molds, mushrooms, and yeasts are not plants.

C. The making of pottery is one of the oldest human endeavors. The term pottery refers to tiles, dishes, vases, and other articles made of baked clay. There are two categories of pottery. The first, and finest, is called porcelain. Porcelain is translucent, meaning that some light can pass through it. The other, earthenware, is opaque, meaning that no light can pass through it.

O Earthenware is a type of pottery.

O Porcelain and earthenware are two types of pottery, or articles made of baked clay.

O True pottery is opaque, meaning no light can pass through it.

Name: _____ **Date:** _____

Here's a tip! Reading isn't just text. Tables, diagrams, labels, or other visual presentations can contain vital information you want or need to know.

Directions: *Everything you need to know to answer the questions is presented visually below. Refer to it to get the information you need.*

MAJOR LEAGUE SOCCER STANDINGS

Western Division	W	L	T	Pts	GF	GA
x-Galaxy	14	7	5	47	52	36
x-San Jose	13	7	6	45	47	29
x-Kansas City	11	13	3	36	33	53
Colorado	5	13	8	23	36	47
Central Division						
y-Chicago	16	6	5	53	50	30
x-Columbus	13	7	6	45	49	36
x-Dallas	10	11	5	35	48	47
Tampa Bay	4	21	2	14	32	68
Eastern Division						
y-Miami	16	5	5	53	57	36
x-New York/New Jersey	13	10	3	42	38	35
New England	7	14	6	27	35	52
D.C. United	8	16	2	26	42	50

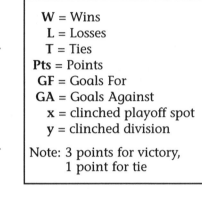

W = Wins
L = Losses
T = Ties
Pts = Points
GF = Goals For
GA = Goals Against
x = clinched playoff spot
y = clinched division

Note: 3 points for victory, 1 point for tie

1. What cities' teams have clinched their divisions? _____

2. What team has had more ties than any other? _____

3. How many teams have had 10 or more losses? _____

4. What city's team has had the most goals scored against them? _____

5. What city's team has made the most goals? _____

6. Of the 12 teams, how many are sure to be in the playoffs? _____

7. Which two teams have the same W-L-T record? _____

8. Which two divisions have the same number of total wins? _____

9. D.C. United won more games than New England. Why are D.C. United's standings higher?

_____

Name: _____ **Date:** _____

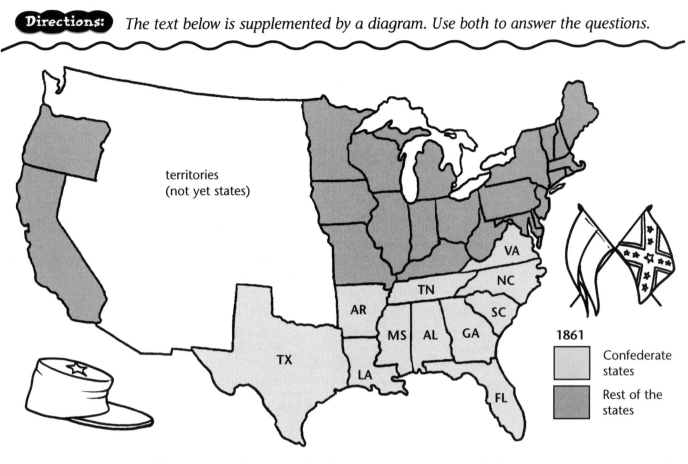

In 1861 there were 33 states. When six southern states organized their own government in February 1861, they took the name Confederate States of America. South Carolina was the first to secede late in 1860. Five others followed early in 1861. By spring, eleven states made up the Confederacy. The main reason for the secession was dispute over the economics of and views about slavery.

1. Name the first state to secede from the Union in 1860. _____

2. Was North Carolina a Confederate state in 1861? _____

3. What three Confederate states were on the border with the North at the time?

   _____ _____ _____

4. How many states were in the Confederacy in 1861? _____

5. Why did the states marked as Confederate withdraw from the Union? _____

   _____

Challenge! Name three current states that were not yet part of the U.S. in 1860.

   _____ _____ _____

Directions: *How do you get information about a product? Check the label! Natalie's city began a recycling program. The city delivered a large container to each home. The label below was attached. Use it to answer the questions.*

HELP US SAVE OUR PLANET

Curbside Recycling
New for Rosewood

The city of Rosewood is providing, free of charge, one large recycling bin per household. Follow the guidelines below for what can and can't be recycled. Then put your bin on the curb each Thursday by 8 AM for pickup.

MATERIAL	EXAMPLES
plastics	containers with #s 1-7, such as milk, soda, and water bottles, butter tubs, styrofoam, and grocery store bags
paper	newspapers, junk mail, phone books, frozen food boxes, pizza boxes, computer paper, cardboard
metal	containers of metal or aluminum, such as drink cans, foil trays, soup cans, and pet food cans; also wire hangers
glass	glass bottles and jars (all colors), soda and juice bottles, and baby food jars

Bottles and jars must be empty and rinsed out. Boxes should be flattened. Lids and labels are OK.

DO NOT INCLUDE
shredded paper, small styrofoam pieces, scrap metal, pots, pans, window glass

If you have any questions call
Rosewood Street Services
389-2341

CITY OF ROSEWOOD

1. How many containers does each household receive? _____
2. How much must each household pay for the container and service? _____
3. Can Natalie put her family's used pizza boxes in the bin? _____
4. Natalie's shampoo bottle is marked with a number 6. Can she recycle it? _____
5. Where should the bin be placed for pickup? _____
6. By what time must the bin be out for pickup? _____
7. What should be done to bottles and jars before placing them in the bin? _____
8. Why do you think they don't want shredded paper or small styrofoam bits? _____
9. Which can be recycled plastic grocery bags, paper grocery bags, neither, or both? _____
10. Who is sponsoring the program and where can they be reached? _____ _____

Name: _____ **Date:** _____

THE NINE MAJOR WORLD CLIMATES

In general, climate is the pattern of weather over a long period of time. Following are nine major climates, based on average temperatures, precipitation, and humidity.

CLIMATE TYPE	TEMPERATURE	PRECIPITATION
Rainy Tropical	hot throughout the year	heavy; distributed evenly throughout year
Wet/Dry Tropical	warm to hot throughout the year	abundant but most during rainy seasons
Semiarid	hot to cold throughout the year	sparse in any season
Desert	hot to cold throughout the year	very sparse; all seasons very dry
Warm Rainy	warm to hot summers, cool winters	ample; well distributed throughout year
Wet/Dry Seasonal	warm to hot summers, cool winters	rainy winter; dry summer
Cool Moist	cold winters, warm to hot summers	medium rain/snow in all seasons
Polar	long, cold winters; short, cool summers	light throughout year; winter snow
Ice Cap	bitter-cold winters, cold summers	very light; frozen throughout year

1. What is the definition of climate? _____

2. What is the difference between Warm Rainy and Wet/Dry Seasonal climate? _____

_____

3. What single term might describe an area that's warm to hot and rainy? _____

4. What's the main difference between Semiarid and Desert? _____

5. What do Ice Cap and Desert climates have in common? _____

6. What general type of climate do you think each of these places has and why?

  a. Alaska: _____

  b. Egypt: _____

  c. Amazon rain forest: _____

  d. Washington, D.C.: _____

- Adult male bee hummingbirds of Cuba can be as small as 2.25" long and weigh only .056 oz.

- The rare whale shark can be 40 ft. long and weigh as much as 20+ tons.

- The largest species of pinniped is the southern elephant seal at up to 20 ft. and 3.5 tons.

- A reticulated python can reach the amazing length of 30 ft. or more.

- A male eastern lowland gorilla can be almost 6 ft. tall and weigh 380 lbs.

- The tiniest true deer is the southern pudu, which may be only 13" at the shoulder and weigh 14 lbs.

- The smallest bat in the U.S. is the western pipistrelle with a wingspan of less than 8".

Some "EST" animals—biggest, smallest

ANIMAL	BIGGEST/LONGEST	SMALLEST/SHORTEST
Pinniped		Galapagos fur seal (~160 lbs.)
Bat	Bismarck flying fox (wingspan 5 ft.+)	
Fish		Dwarf pygmy gobi (1/3 in. long, <.0002 oz.)
Deer	Alaskan moose (1500 lbs.+)	
Primate		Rufus mouse lemur (< 3 oz.)
Bird	Ostrich (330 lbs.+)	
Snake		Martinique thread snake (pencil lead thickness)

Name: _____   **Date:** _____

Always question yourself as you read. Train yourself to sort the information you read as: important or not important. It works like a charm!

Directions: *Circle the letter of the sentence that does not belong in a paragraph with the rest. Be prepared to explain your choices.*

1. Which does not belong in a paragraph about shrews?

   a. Shrews are mouselike mammals.

   b. There are about 200 species of shrews.

   c. Shrews are not as cute as mice.

   d. Most are land-dwellers, but some are aquatic.

2. Which does not belong in a paragraph about gibbons?

   a. Asia is home to many wild animals.

   b. Gibbons make their homes in rain forests.

   c. They live in the trees where there is food and shelter.

   d. Gibbons eat fruits, nuts, seeds, leaves, insects, and sometimes young birds.

3. Which does not belong in a paragraph about kookaburras?

   a. A kookaburra is an Australian bird.

   b. Holes in trees are where kookaburras like to make their homes.

   c. Their favorite food is insects, but they also eat fish, frogs, and worms.

   d. There is a fun-to-sing song about the Kookaburra.

4. Which does not belong in a paragraph about insects?

   a. An insect has three main body parts—head, thorax, and abdomen.

   b. A spider is not an insect.

   c. An insect's body is protected by an exoskeleton—a hard covering.

   d. All adult insects have six legs.

5. Which does not belong in a paragraph about guinea pigs?

   a. Guinea pigs are rodents, not pigs.

   b. Their teeth never stop growing, so guinea pigs must gnaw on wood or other material to keep them worn down.

   c. Guinea pigs make good pets.

   d. Like other nocturnal animals, guinea pigs are most active at night.

Name: _____   **Date:** _____

1. The Scissors, Paper, Stone game was first played in Japan.

_____

2. The Japanese counterpart of Paper is Po.

_____

3. If one person shows stone and the other scissors, the person showing stone is the winner.

_____

4. A clenched fist is the symbol for scissors.

_____

5. The game must be played by only two participants.

_____

6. With practice, you could figure out a strategy for winning more often than your partner.

_____

7. The players must extend their hands showing their symbols at exactly the same time.

_____

8. Scissors, Paper, Stone and Jan Ken Po are the same game.

_____

Scissors, Paper, Stone

The well-known and popular game of Scissors, Paper, Stone originated in Japan, where it is called Jan Ken Po.

The game is played in pairs. The players count to three as they pound their fist into their hand. Then, simultaneously, each player extends a hand showing one of the symbols below.

scissors: middle and index finger extended

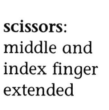

paper: hand held out flat

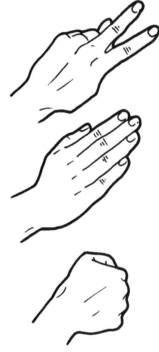

stone: clenched fist

The winner is determined by the following rules:

- scissors cuts paper
- paper covers stone
- stone breaks scissors

This game can be used to break a tie, settle a difference of opinion, or just for fun. Why not try it with a friend?

Name: _____ **Date:** _____

A Tasteful Gift

Christine received an unusual birthday gift from her friend, Michelle. It was a clear glass jar filled with flour, salt, baking soda, white sugar, brown sugar, and chocolate candies. A small wooden mixing spoon was attached to the lid of the jar with some twine. On the lid of the jar were these instructions:

In addition, you will need: 2 sticks of softened butter, 1 egg, and 1 tablespoon of vanilla extract. After you have gathered these additional ingredients, empty the jar contents into a mixing bowl. Use the spoon to mix. In a separate bowl, blend the butter, vanilla, and egg together. Add the dry ingredients to the butter, vanilla, and egg mixture. Stir well. Using the spoon, place a dozen dollops onto a baking sheet. Bake at 350 degrees for eight to ten minutes. Centers will be soft. Makes about three dozen.

Christine asked her mother to help her make the tasty treats and when they were done, she invited Michelle over to have a taste of the birthday gift she had given her.

_____ 1. Christine's birthday was in May.

_____ 2. A small wooden spoon was included with the jar of ingredients.

_____ 3. Two bowls were needed to make the recipe.

_____ 4. Christine's mother had the additional ingredients needed in her kitchen.

_____ 5. The mix would yield about three dozen treats.

_____ 6. Michelle had given Christine a chocolate chip cookie mix.

_____ 7. Together, Christine and Michelle enjoyed the birthday treat.

☐ The Komodo dragon is the largest living lizard.

☐ It exists today only on a few small islands of Indonesia, including Komodo.

☐ Lizards are in the reptile family.

☐ This great reptile can reach a length of 10 feet and weigh 250 pounds.

☐ It has a long tail and its body is covered with small scales.

☐ Turtles, alligators, and crocodiles are also lizards.

☐ The Komodo dragon has sharp eyesight and a keen sense of smell.

☐ Its size, strength, and powerful claws and teeth make it a fearsome hunter.

☐ Another animal with "dragon" in its name is the dragonfly.

☐ Komodo dragons hunt during the day and rest at night.

☐ This species is a member of the most ancient group of lizards alive today.

☐ Some dinosaurs were lizards.

Name: _____   **Date:** _____

You probably pick movies by type—comedy, drama, action. Stories, too, are classified by type, or genre. For more reading savvy, learn to recognize these.

Directions: *One type of story genre is folklore. Folklore includes such types of stories as myths, fairy tales, legends, fables, and tall tales. Learn the differences below. Then read the story and answer the questions.*

Myth: explains the forces of nature; often by way of gods and goddesses
Fairy Tale: contains supernatural beings or events; for entertainment
Legend: based on real people but exaggerated events and actions
Fable: animals or people teach a moral, or lesson, for living
Tall Tale: features humor and overly exaggerated acts of heroism

Belling the Cat

A large family of mice lived in Farmer Jack's barn. There was plenty to eat (grain and corn) and room to play in the fields. The mice could have lived very happily and comfortably except for one thing. Farmer Jack had a cat.

Many cats are known to sleep all day and not bother with such trivial things as a family of mice. But not this cat. He was keenly interested in mice and would love to make one or two his meal.

The mice lived in fear. Each knew that at any moment the cat might pounce on one of them. The eldest mouse called a council meeting. Each mouse was to offer ideas on how to solve the cat problem.

The mice were silent as they pondered how they could outwit their enemy. At last, one spoke up. He explained that the problem was that the cat could sneak up on them. If they put a bell on his neck, they would hear him coming and be able to escape.

Everyone cheered at the idea, except the eldest mouse. He wrinkled his nose and sighed. The others looked at him puzzled. "Yes," he said slowly, "belling the cat is a good idea. But there's just one problem. Which of you is going to do it?"

All the mice lowered their heads, realizing that many things are easier said than done.

1. Which specific type of folklore is this story? _____

2. What clues led you to your conclusion? _____

_____

3. Why isn't it a myth? _____ a fairy tale? _____

_____ a legend? _____

4. What is the moral of the story? _____

Name: _____ **Date:** _____

There are really only two types of stories, fact and fiction. Any story that is not fact-based (such as a biography) is fiction. Think about the different kinds of fiction below. Then use the clues in the story excerpt to identify what specific kind of fiction it is.

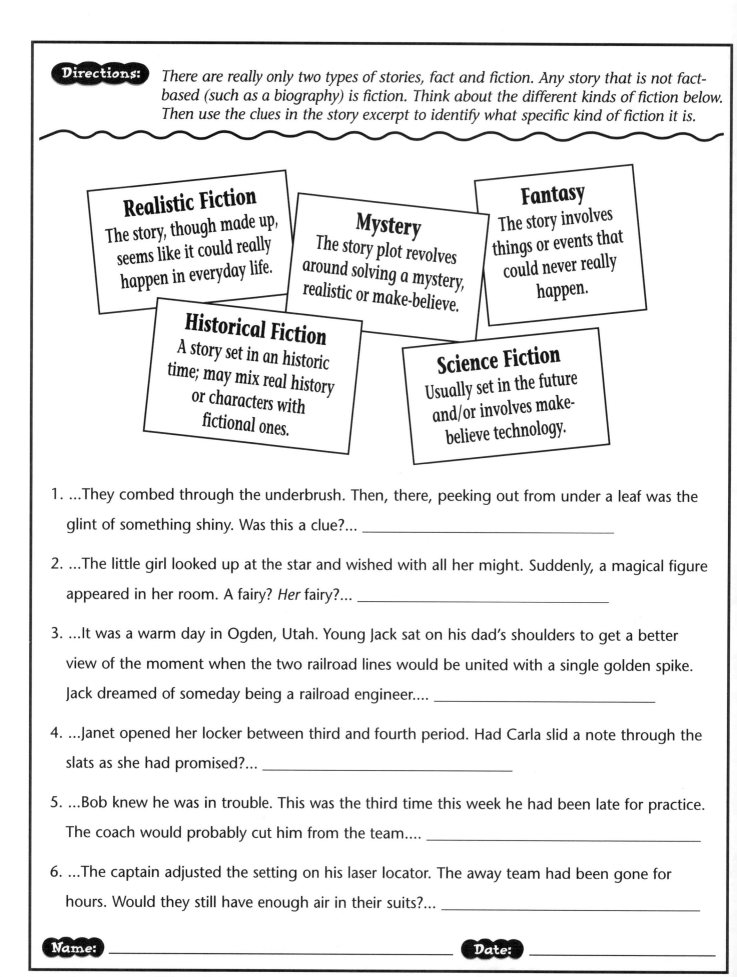

Realistic Fiction
The story, though made up, seems like it could really happen in everyday life.

Mystery
The story plot revolves around solving a mystery, realistic or make-believe.

Fantasy
The story involves things or events that could never really happen.

Historical Fiction
A story set in an historic time; may mix real history or characters with fictional ones.

Science Fiction
Usually set in the future and/or involves make-believe technology.

1. ...They combed through the underbrush. Then, there, peeking out from under a leaf was the glint of something shiny. Was this a clue?... _____

2. ...The little girl looked up at the star and wished with all her might. Suddenly, a magical figure appeared in her room. A fairy? *Her* fairy?... _____

3. ...It was a warm day in Ogden, Utah. Young Jack sat on his dad's shoulders to get a better view of the moment when the two railroad lines would be united with a single golden spike. Jack dreamed of someday being a railroad engineer.... _____

4. ...Janet opened her locker between third and fourth period. Had Carla slid a note through the slats as she had promised?... _____

5. ...Bob knew he was in trouble. This was the third time this week he had been late for practice. The coach would probably cut him from the team.... _____

6. ...The captain adjusted the setting on his laser locator. The away team had been gone for hours. Would they still have enough air in their suits?... _____

Folklore-Legend
Folklore-Myth
Folklore-Fable
Folklore-Fairy Tale
Folklore-Tall Tale

Science Fiction
Realistic Fiction
Historical Fiction
Fantasy
Mystery

_____ 1. story set in historic time; may mix real characters with fictional

_____ 2. story that contains supernatural beings or events, such as fairies

_____ 3. a story that seems like it could really happen in everyday life

_____ 4. tale that explains the forces of nature, often by way of gods

_____ 5. story involving fantastic things or events that could never happen

_____ 6. usually set in the future and/or involves make-believe technology

_____ 7. story in which animals or people teach a lesson for living

_____ 8. features humor and overly exaggerated acts of heroism

_____ 9. story with a plot that revolves around solving a mystery

_____ 10. tale based on real people but exaggerated events and actions

Story Genre

Example (title and brief description)

(sample) Fantasy   Jumanji: a game comes alive

1._____   _____

2._____   _____

3._____   _____

4._____   _____

Directions: *Read each sentence. Identify it as the topic sentence or as a supporting sentence. Write TS or SS.*

(A)

_____ 1. *Kinetic* is the energy of motion and action, such as blowing up a balloon.

_____ 2. Energy is described as one of two types—kinetic and potential.

_____ 3. *Potential* is the energy that is stored with the potential for causing action, such as holding your breath.

(B)

_____ 1. Cactus plants are specially adapted to get water in arid environments.

_____ 2. Their roots are very shallow and cover a large area.

_____ 3. This helps the cactus collect as much water as possible from the soil.

(C)

_____ 1. Properties include color, size, shape, hardness, and even taste.

_____ 2. Some kinds of properties can be measured, while others cannot.

_____ 3. Property is a way of describing matter.

(D)

_____ 1. A prairie dog "town" is made up of many families of prairie dogs.

_____ 2. Each family has one adult male, from one to four females, and several young.

_____ 3. Up to a thousand or more prairie dogs may live in a single "town."

Name: _____   **Date:** _____

1. The spider monkey is a small and agile member of the primate family.

   _____

2. A zebra can run as fast as 45 miles per hour.

   _____

3. Beetles can be both helpful and harmful to farmers.

   _____

4. Alligators differ from crocodiles in a number of ways.

   _____

5. Every tiger claims its own territory.

   _____

6. The horse's teeth never stop growing.

   _____

7. Frogs can take in water through their skin.

   _____

8. Whales are divided into two groups—toothed and baleen.

   _____

9. Sloths rarely venture down onto the ground.

   _____

10. The toucan is a variety of bird known for its large colorful bill.

    _____

11. Giant pandas feed mainly on bamboo.

    _____

12. Of the seventeen kinds of penguins, the Emperor penguin is the largest.

    _____

Camels

- Their feet are well adapted for walking on sand with ease.
- The Arabian camel has one hump: the Bactrian camel two.
- The humps are stores of fat that camels can draw upon for energy when food is scarce.
- The humps enable camels to travel hundreds of miles on little food and water.
- They can carry people and supplies where there are no roads.

The camel is a large desert animal commonly used in Africa and Asia for work and transportation. _____

_____

_____

_____

_____

There are two main types of camels. _____

_____

_____

_____

_____

_____

_____

Reading Comprehension • Saddleback Publishing, Inc. ©2002   86   3 Watson, Irvine, CA 92618•Phone (888)SDL-BACK• www.sdlback.com

You may think there were no lamps before Edison invented the electric light about 125 years ago. But there have been forms of lamps since prehistoric times.

The first lamps may have been brush set afire in an animal skull filled with fat. Later, but still thousands of years ago, Egyptians placed cotton wicks inside hollow stones filled with grease. Greeks and Romans shaped lamps from bronze or terra cotta and used olive oil for fuel. Candles were a great improvement when they appeared. In the 1700s the discovery that under glass a flame burns more brightly and with less smoke led to glass encasements. Whale oil was the main source of fuel at this time until scientists learned to use gas as a fuel. In the 1800s, kerosene lamps appeared on the scene. Prior to Edison's invention, gaslight lamps were widely used. They were not only functional but also sometimes ornate decorations for the home.

1 Write the topic sentence. _____

_____

2. What was used as fuel in the first lamps?

   O gas   O animal fat   O olive oil

3. During what period did candles appear as a source of light?

   O prehistoric   O 1800s   O story doesn't say

4. During the 1700s, what was the main source of fuel in lamps?

   O whale oil   O olive oil   O grease

5. About what year did Edison invent the electric light?

   O 1775   O 1823   O 1879

6. Who invented the gaslight lamp?

   O Greeks and Romans   O Edison   O story doesn't say

Reading Comprehension • Saddleback Publishing, Inc. ©2002   87   3 Watson, Irvine, CA 92618•Phone (888)SDL-BACK• www.sdlback.com

A Tale of Two Pharaohs

Tutankhamen was pharaoh of Egypt from 1333-1323 B.C. Having such a short reign and being so young (he died at 18), King Tut was a minor figure among pharaohs in Egypt's long history. He contributed nothing of great importance to Egypt in his time, yet, in modern times, he is credited with supplying an enormous amount of information about ancient Egyptian culture. It was not in life that Tutankhamen made his mark in history, but in death.

In 1922, Tutankhamen's tomb was discovered by Howard Carter, an Englishman. Somehow, Tut's tomb escaped rampage for more than 3,000 years. Tut was found just as he was placed—enclosed in a solid gold sarcophagus, along with all the magnificent trappings of a king. The huge amount and excellent condition of the artifacts provided us with valuable knowledge about the life and times of ancient Egypt.

Another well-known pharaoh of ancient Egypt is Ramses II, who ruled from 1279–1212 B.C. At a time when people were on average five feet tall and lived only a few decades, Ramses was 6 feet tall, lived to be 90, and ruled for some 67 years. He is known as Ramses the Great because during his reign he asserted his power for the glory of Egypt and built a new capital and many great temples.

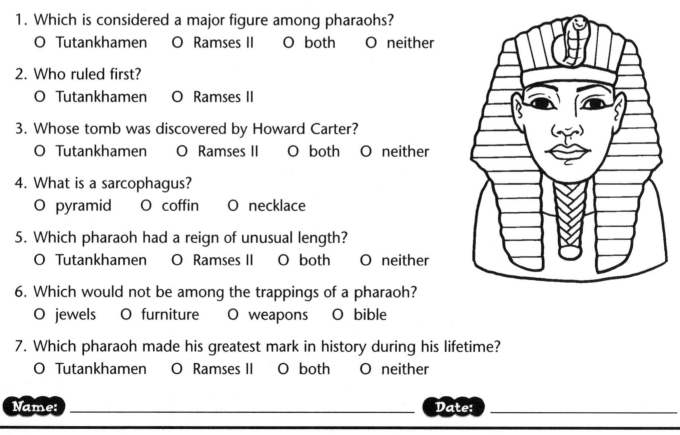

1. Which is considered a major figure among pharaohs?
   O Tutankhamen   O Ramses II   O both   O neither

2. Who ruled first?
   O Tutankhamen   O Ramses II

3. Whose tomb was discovered by Howard Carter?
   O Tutankhamen   O Ramses II   O both   O neither

4. What is a sarcophagus?
   O pyramid   O coffin   O necklace

5. Which pharaoh had a reign of unusual length?
   O Tutankhamen   O Ramses II   O both   O neither

6. Which would not be among the trappings of a pharaoh?
   O jewels   O furniture   O weapons   O bible

7. Which pharaoh made his greatest mark in history during his lifetime?
   O Tutankhamen   O Ramses II   O both   O neither

Name: _____   **Date:** _____

Almost any two things have similarities and differences. Compare and contrast is just a fancy way of asking how are things alike and different.

Think about each pair of things below—their properties, uses, shapes—any defining description. Then write one way the two are alike and one way they are different.

EXAMPLE:

nest, hive alike: <u>Both are homes for wild creatures.</u>

different: <u>A nest is built by birds, a hive is built by bees or wasps.</u>

1. **planet, moon**

    alike: _____

    different: _____

2. **elephant, mouse**

    alike: _____

    different: _____

3. **map, globe**

    alike: _____

    different: _____

4. **wallet, purse**

    alike: _____

    different: _____

5. **wool, cotton**

    alike: _____

    different: _____

6. **office, school**

    alike: _____

    different: _____

7. **clock, thermometer**

    alike: _____

    different: _____

Name: _____   **Date:** _____

Directions: *Below is part of the information on the labels of two over-the-counter cold medicines—a cough syrup and cough drops. Compare and contrast them.*

COLD-AID Cough & Congestion Syrup

Maximum Strength, Non-Drowsy Formula

USES: *Temporarily relieves*
- cough
- nasal congestion due to colds

DIRECTIONS: *Use teaspoon (tsp.)*
Ask doctor before giving to children under 6 yrs.

6-11 yrs. (48-95 lbs.)	1 ½ tsp.
12 yrs. and up (over 95 lbs.)	3 tsp.

Repeat every 6 hours, not to exceed 4 doses per day, or as directed by doctor.

WARNINGS: If nervousness, dizziness, or sleeplessness occur, discontinue use and consult doctor.

ACTIVE INGREDIENTS
(per 3 teaspoons)
Dextromethorphan HBr 30 mg.
Pseudoephedrine HCl 60 mg.
Alcohol 5%

COLD-AID Cough Lozenges

Regular Strength, Wild Cherry Flavor

USES: *For temporary relief of minor irritation, pain, and sore mouth or throat.*

DIRECTIONS:
Adults and children 2 yrs. and older:
Allow one lozenge to dissolve slowly in the mouth. May be repeated every 2 hours as needed or as directed by doctor or dentist.
Children under 2 yrs. consult a doctor or dentist.

WARNINGS: If sore throat is severe or persists for more than 2 days, is accompanied or followed by fever, headache, rash, swelling, or nausea, discontinue use and consult a doctor.

ACTIVE INGREDIENTS
Each lozenge contains
Dyclonine Hyrdochloride 2 mg.
Also contains Corn Syrup, FD&C Blue 1, FD&C Red 40, Flavor, Mineral Oil, Silicon Dioxide, Sucrose, Tartaric Acid.

1. Do both products do the same thing? _____

2. Which product contains alcohol? _____

3. If you were 11 years old but weighed 100 pounds, what dosage would you take of the syrup?
_____

4. Are the active ingredients in the two products the same or different? _____

5. Compare the advertised strength of the two products._____
_____

6. Compare the dose frequency of the two products. _____

7. How are the two products' warnings alike and different? _____
_____

8. Which of these products would you take or not take and why? _____
_____

Name: _____   **Date:** _____

The **great white shark** is larger, faster, and more dangerous than most. It can reach a length of 20 feet and weigh 70,000 pounds. Though its preferred diet is seals and dolphins, this fearsome fish regularly attacks almost any type of warm-blooded animal. In its snout are small holes that lead to receptors. These receptors pick up electrical nerve signals in the prey. The shark also has other sensors that detect blood in the water. Very rare in tropical or polar regions, great whites patrol mainly temperate ocean coastlines.

The body is designed for efficiency in the water. It is broad in the middle and tapered at the ends for streamlined movement. Winglike pectoral fins provide lift and stability. An oil stored in the liver adds buoyancy. The tail fins are vertical and act as a rudder for fast turns. Amazingly it never stops swimming.

All sharks are fish and most are carnivores. The great white is the world's largest predatory shark. The whale shark is nearly twice as big, but like a baleen whale, eats mainly plankton.

The **blue whale** is the largest known mammal to ever live. Its size ranges from 70 to 100 feet in length and up to 125 tons in weight (250,000 pounds). Despite its enormity, the blue whale lives on krill, a tiny crustacean, and other planktonic organisms. An adult ingests 3-4 tons of krill per day. This is done by scooping up large quantities of water containing krill with its huge mouth. In its mouth are not teeth, but rather a series of sheets, similar in consistency to our fingernails, that serve as a filtering system. These sheets, or baleen, grow from the roof of the mouth, ranging from smooth to brushlike. The blue whale lives in the open ocean but tends to migrate to the polar waters in spring and back to subtropical waters in fall.

In water, the weight of the body is not as much a factor as the shape. Like sharks, whales have torpedo-shaped bodies and pectoral fins for balance. Their tail fins, however, are horizontal, which is more suited for forward motion rather than making sharp turns.

Blue whales have been hunted relentlessly in the past for their blubber and oil. As a result they were nearly hunted to extinction and still remain on the endangered animal list.

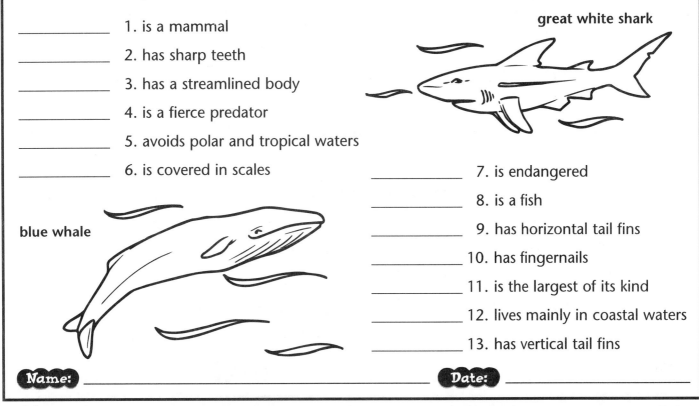

_____ 1. is a mammal

_____ 2. has sharp teeth

_____ 3. has a streamlined body

_____ 4. is a fierce predator

_____ 5. avoids polar and tropical waters

_____ 6. is covered in scales

great white shark

blue whale

_____ 7. is endangered

_____ 8. is a fish

_____ 9. has horizontal tail fins

_____ 10. has fingernails

_____ 11. is the largest of its kind

_____ 12. lives mainly in coastal waters

_____ 13. has vertical tail fins

Name: _____   **Date:** _____

Valeen enjoys spending time with her grandmother. Valeen is fascinated with the stories Grandma tells about how things have changed since she was a girl. Read one of her stories below. Then answer the questions.

When I was a little girl growing up in the 1940s, we didn't have much in the way of material things. The Great Depression had hit just about everyone, and we were just climbing out of it. My dad had a job at a factory, and mom stayed at home with the kids. I got a new outfit once a year, and that was only because Mom was pretty good with the sewing machine. Good thing, too, because when World War II came, Mom got a job sewing uniforms for the soldiers. The extra money helped, and by the time I was in my teens in the late 1950s we had enough to get one of those fancy new television sets. It was black and white and only got three channels, but we were glued to it.

I decided around that time that I didn't want to work in a factory or sew like my mom had. I wanted to go to college. A girl aspiring to a career at that time raised some eyebrows. Worse still, I wanted to be a lawyer. Though others scoffed, my parents told me that they would support me in any way they could.

Fortunately, I worked hard at school and got a scholarship. It wasn't easy, but a few years later I was a lawyer.

At first I was a little overwhelmed. But in the late '60s I knew I could use my education and spirit to help our nation. I took a job working against discrimination as a civil rights attorney. That's where I met your Grandpa. He was not only handsome but believed in the same things I did and still do—equality and justice. When your mom came along, I took a year off but went right back to work. We were able to afford a color TV and, like me, your mom was glued to it. She had an intense interest not in the programs, but how the thing worked. I guess I knew from the time she was watching "Sesame Street" that she would also take a path that was not normally taken by women. She became an electrician.

So, Valeen, I wonder what's left for you to try that is uncharted territory for women. After all, it seems to run in our family.

1. Name a way Valeen's mother and grandmother were alike. _____
_____

2. Compare Valeen's grandparents to her great-grandparents. _____
_____

3. What did Grandma mean by "raised some eyebrows"? _____
_____

4. Today college enrollment is roughly equal between men and women. Are there any fields
   you think are still "uncharted territory" for women? _____

5. Contrast Valeen's opportunities today to that of her grandmother's as a teen. _____
_____

Name: _____   **Date:** _____

Work with a partner to do this compare and contrast activity. First, interview your partner. Write down his or her answers to the interview questionnaire. Then, use both your answers to list ways you are alike and different.

Name _____ Age _____ Birthday _____

Family _____

_____ Pets? _____

Favorites: color _____ book _____

movie _____ sport _____

animal _____ music/song _____

school subject _____ (fill in your own) _____

Hobbies/Interests: _____

_____

Top three pet peeves: _____

_____

What you are really good at: _____

What you are really not good at: _____

What you'd like to be doing in 10 years: _____

Ways _____ and I are ALIKE   Ways _____ and I are DIFFERENT

_____   _____

_____   _____

_____   _____

_____   _____

_____   _____

_____   _____

_____   _____

_____   _____

Name: _____   **Date:** _____

I, Pauline, am an only child and I love it. First, when I was little I got all the attention. My grandparents, and even my parents to some extent, spoiled me. I got more presents and toys than I would have if I had brothers and sisters. Next, growing up we never had to schedule around kids' activities. I was it, so no waiting or giving up something or other because a brother or sister had a conflict or "dibs." Third, I always had my own room all to myself. There were no bigger or younger brothers and sisters to mess with my stuff or borrow things from me. Finally, and maybe best of all, I never had to stay home to watch a brother or sister or drag them along with me somewhere.

I, Dale, have an older brother and a younger sister, and I love being the middle child of three. First, there's always someone around to do things with, even if it's just watching TV. Second, in addition to all the stuff I have, there's my brother's and sister's stuff, too. Whatever I want or need is usually available to use or borrow. Third, having a brother and sister means there is always someone to talk to who understands what it's like to be a kid. We help each other with all kinds of things from homework to putting a united front on to the parents when we want something. Finally, and best of all, there are three of us to do the chores around the house, and we can even trade if we want to.

1. What do Pauline and Dale share in common? _____

   _____

2. Each person exalts the advantages of their situation and ignores the disadvantages.

   One disadvantage Dale could point out to Pauline about being an only child is that it can be

   lonely. Name another. _____

   One disadvantage Pauline could point out to Dale about having siblings is that there is little

   or no privacy. Name another. _____

3. Pauline and Dale have opposing views. Is one right and one wrong? Why or why not? _____

   _____

4. If you had to trade places with Pauline or Dale, which would you choose? _____

5. Describe your own situation: Are you an only child or do you have siblings? If you do, how

   many and where do you fall in the age range?_____

6. Are you happy with your situation as Pauline and Dale are, or would you rather it was a

   different way? Give your views and explain why. _____

   _____

Reading Comprehension • Saddleback Publishing, Inc. ©2002   94   3 Watson, Irvine, CA 92618•Phone (888)SDL-BACK• www.sdlback.com

Directions: *Write a phrase from the box at the right to tell what most likely happened as a result of the action.*

1. Diane woke up with a stomach ache this morning, so _____ _____

- she was absent from school today.
- she felt better later.
- she walked to school rather than take the bus.

2. John is allergic to peanuts so _____ _____ _____

- he checks the ingredients in what he eats.
- he never eats any candy or sandwiches.
- he eats only homemade foods.

3. Neil promised to call his friend back but he forgot so_____ _____

- he offered his friend ten dollars.
- his friend never spoke to him again.
- he apologized to his friend.

4. Mr. Gates is trying to lose a little weight so _____ _____

- he takes the stairs instead of the elevator.
- he quit his job to work out 8 hours a day.
- he bought all new clothes.

5. Pam missed several math problems on her last test so _____ _____

- she did well on her English test.
- she stayed after school for some extra help.
- she hired a private teacher.

6. Vicky did not have enough money with her to buy lunch so _____ _____

- she lost it on the way to school.
- she borrowed some from a friend.
- she ate some apples off a tree.

Name: _____   **Date:** _____

It was test day in Mr. Koch's class. Everyone was busy reading and filling in answers on their test papers. Suddenly Richard gasped. He had seen something move, no scurry, across the classroom floor from the corner of his eye. Or had he? He thought perhaps he just imagined it, and went back to concentrating on his test. Then, a moment later, there it went again, this time in the other direction, toward the door. He still wasn't sure what he'd seen, but he was sure he had seen something. He considered telling Mr. Koch, but thought better than to disturb the group during a test.

He tried to keep his mind focused on identifying the parts of speech in the passage he was reading, but it kept returning to the "thing" he saw. "What if it was rat?" he thought with distaste and concern. Unlikely he decided...but not impossible. He found himself scanning the floor every few seconds in hopes of catching another glimpse of it and settling his imagination down into reality.

It did not reappear the rest of the period. At lunch he told his friends about the mystery sighting and his fears that it could have been a rat, or a mouse at the very least. The school could be infested! At that suggestion, a few of them automatically raised their feet and looked down. Marj just sat there with a wide grin. She let them speculate for awhile, then told them how one of the hamsters kept in Miss Moore's room had gotten loose that morning, but came back to the room shortly after his adventure.

1. What caused Richard to gasp? _____

2. Why did Richard doubt that he really saw something? _____

_____

3. What event caused Richard to be sure he had seen something ? _____

_____

4. What thought caused Richard concern? _____

5. Why did Richard decide to not alert Mr. Koch? _____

6. What suggestion caused Richard's friends to react by raising their feet? _____

_____

7. Why did Marj react with a smile instead? _____

8. What was the mystery? _____

Name: _____   Date: _____

How are story characters like snowflakes? Every one is different! Explore the many sides of characters to get more from the stories you read.

Directions: *Below is an unusual type of crossword puzzle. Each clue is a character from a well-known story. The missing word in the puzzle is a word that describes that character. The trait box will help you choose the right ones.*

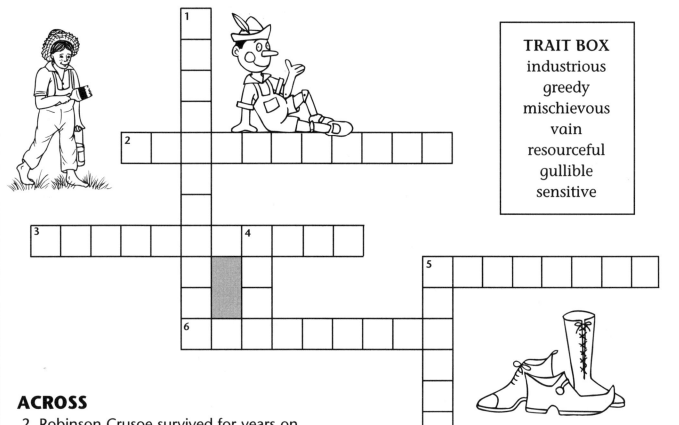

TRAIT BOX
industrious
greedy
mischievous
vain
resourceful
gullible
sensitive

ACROSS

2. Robinson Crusoe survived for years on a deserted island and was unusually
   _____.

3. Pinocchio wanted to be a good boy, but he couldn't seem to help being
   _____.

5. Tom Sawyer was able to get Ben to whitewash the fence because Ben was
   _____.

6. By noticing a single pea under twenty mattresses, the girl showed she was
   _____ enough to be a princess.

DOWN

1. The _____ elves worked all night to make shoes for the old shoemaker and his wife.

4. The _____ Emperor loved nothing more than fine clothes (except maybe himself) and so would not admit that he couldn't see the magic cloth.

5. No matter how many wishes she was granted, the _____ fisherman's wife was not satisfied.

Name: _____ **Date:** _____

Name	Character Traits	Problem	Resolution
Dorothy	1. 2. 3.		
Lion	1. 2. 3.		
Tin Man	1. 2. 3.		
Scarecrow	1. 2. 3.		

The character of the Wizard had two sides—what Dorothy and her friends perceived him to be and what he really was. Explain. _____

_____

_____

_____

_____

 Name: _____   **Date:** _____

Keep this in mind: How something seems depends on from where and when you see it. In other words, your perspective depends upon your point of view.

Directions: *Stories are often set in times other than the present. To understand and appreciate the story, you should be aware of the chronology, or relative time frame. Use the timeline below to study key time points. Place the story in the correct year and tell why.*

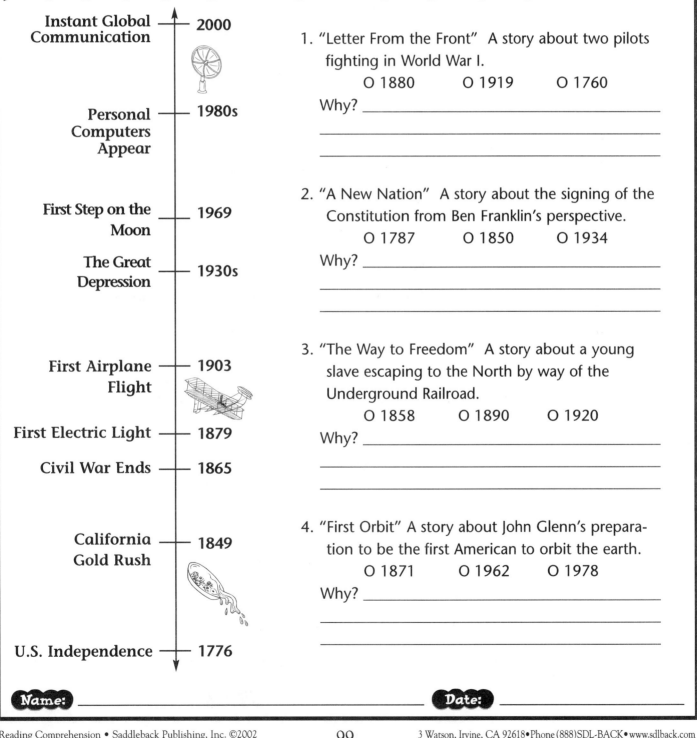

Instant Global Communication — 2000

Personal Computers Appear — 1980s

First Step on the Moon — 1969

The Great Depression — 1930s

First Airplane Flight — 1903

First Electric Light — 1879

Civil War Ends — 1865

California Gold Rush — 1849

U.S. Independence — 1776

1. "Letter From the Front" A story about two pilots fighting in World War I.
   O 1880   O 1919   O 1760
   Why? _____
   _____
   _____

2. "A New Nation" A story about the signing of the Constitution from Ben Franklin's perspective.
   O 1787   O 1850   O 1934
   Why? _____
   _____
   _____

3. "The Way to Freedom" A story about a young slave escaping to the North by way of the Underground Railroad.
   O 1858   O 1890   O 1920
   Why? _____
   _____
   _____

4. "First Orbit" A story about John Glenn's preparation to be the first American to orbit the earth.
   O 1871   O 1962   O 1978
   Why? _____
   _____
   _____

Name: _____   **Date:** _____

Imagine that a reporter is interviewing characters from the story "Goldilocks and the Three Bears." Answer the questions as you think each character would.

GOLDILOCKS

Q. What prompted you to enter the Bears' house?

A. _____

Q. Some are saying that you should not have gone in, even if the door was open. How do you respond to this criticism?

A. _____

Q. When you saw the porridge on the table, where did you think the house's residents were?

A. _____

FATHER BEAR

Q. The people want to know why you left the house when porridge was just set on the table.

A. _____

Q. Looking back, do you think it was foolish to leave the door unlatched?

A. _____

Q. What action, if any, do you think should be taken against Goldilocks for trespassing?

A. _____

MOTHER BEAR

Q. What was your first thought when you saw that the house had been tampered with?

A. _____

Q. What are you going to do about the damage to the furniture?

A. _____

BABY BEAR

Q. How did you feel when you saw Goldilocks asleep in your bed?

A. _____

Q. What lesson do you think your family has learned from this experience?

A. _____

Name: _____   **Date:** _____

Directions: *People often have different opinions about a subject based on their knowledge, beliefs, experience, or what they've been told. It is important that you not only express your opinions, but see the opposite as well. On this page you will take a challenge. First, for each subject, give your opinion and reasons for it. Then present the opposite view.*

SUBJECT 1: Having a set allowance vs. asking for money as needed.

Which do you think is better? Why?

_____

_____

_____

_____

Now take the opposite view. Give reasons why <u>it</u> is better.

_____

_____

_____

_____

SUBJECT 2: Being an only child vs. having one or more siblings

Which do you think is better? Why?

_____

_____

_____

_____

Now take the opposite view. Give reasons why <u>it</u> is better.

_____

_____

_____

_____

Name: _____ **Date:** _____

A. *(from a furniture store)*

Find storewide exceptional savings.

_____

B. *(from a computer store)*

Plenty of power, affordable price

_____

C. *(from a builder)*

We'll beat any written estimate.

_____

D. *(from toy store)*

Save 30–50% on stuffed animals.

_____

E. *(from an eye care center)*

Buy one pair, get the second at $\frac{1}{2}$ price.

_____

F. *(from a cleaning service)*

The best value for your money.

_____

G. *(from a jewelry store)*

Pay no interest for 6 months.

_____

H. *(from a restaurant)*

Free dessert with every kid's meal.

_____

I. *(from a carpet store)*

It adds color and warmth to your home.

_____

Name: _____   **Date:** _____

Directions: *Imagine that you are on a committee of students and teachers planning a fundraiser for your school. The committee came up with several ideas. Then they took an opinion poll among the total student body. This chart shows the results. Use it to help you answer the questions.*

	First Graders	Second Graders	Third Graders	Fourth Graders	Fifth Graders	Sixth Graders	Teachers
Have a bake sale	8	9	12	7	8	5	3
Sell used toys and books	22	14	9	10	12	6	8
Hold a family field day	10	6	11	21	14	17	5
Put on a talent show	2	11	5	10	23	21	1
Host a spaghetti dinner	12	14	17	8	11	9	3

1. In the teachers' opinion, what idea is least popular?_____

2. Which event got the most total votes? _____

3. Which group likes selling toys and books most? _____

4. What two grades overwhelmingly favor a talent show? _____

5. What are the total votes for each idea: bake sale _____ sell toys _____

   field day _____ talent show _____ spaghetti dinner _____

6. Do you think any group's opinion should carry more weight than the others?

   _____ Why? _____

7. Which idea do you think would raise the most money? _____

8. Which idea would you vote for? _____ Why? _____

   _____

9. After reviewing the data, what would your recommendation to the committee be

   and why? _____

   _____

Reading Comprehension • Saddleback Publishing, Inc. ©2002   3 Watson, Irvine, CA 92618•Phone (888)SDL-BACK•www.sdlback.com

☐ The woman is creating a sculpture.

☐ She is using a power-assisted chisel.

☐ The woman is wearing heavy gloves to protect her hands.

☐ The woman does sculpture for a living, not just a hobby.

☐ She is concentrating on what she is doing.

☐ The woman works long hours.

☐ The woman has a workshop in her home.

☐ She has many other tools.

☐ Safety goggles protect her eyes from flying bits.

☐ The woman enjoys her work.

☐ Her finished piece will be displayed in a gallery.

☐ This is not her first sculpting project.

Close Quarters

I live in an apartment complex in the city. It's about two blocks from my school. My building has six floors, and from my bedroom window at the top I can see the little city park in the next block. The greatest thing about living here is that my best friend lives in my building, too. I don't care if it's raining or snowing, all I have to do is walk down a flight of stairs to see her. I meet her every morning, and we walk to school together and then back home.

I don't think I would like living out in the country or even in the suburbs. It would be lonely!

1. On what floor of the apartment building does the writer live? _____
   How can you tell?_____

2. Was the writer's best friend a boy or girl? _____ How can you tell?_____
   _____

3. Of these two choices, which is more likely to be the writer's home city:
   Chicago, Illinois, or San Diego, California? _____ Why? _____
   _____

4. What is the writer's opinion about living in an apartment building? _____
   _____

5. Do you think the writer has ever lived in the country or suburbs? _____
   What makes you think so? _____

6. Would the writer rather live in the city or suburbs? _____ Why?_____
   _____

7. What does the title "Close Quarters" mean? _____
   _____
   Does the writer use it in a positive or negative way? _____

Directions: *It can be helpful to formulate some questions before you read to help you focus on the details. Read the questions below before you read the passage. Then go back and answer them.*

1. Name five different types of objects in our solar system: _____

_____ _____ _____ _____

2. How many stars are in our solar system? _____

3. What well-known comet will reappear in the year 2061? _____

4. What is a meteor? _____

5. Name a natural satellite of Earth. _____

6. Where is the asteroid belt located? _____

You may think of our solar system as just our sun, the only star, and the nine known planets. But other things are in the solar system, too.

First, there are many satellites. A satellite is any small body orbiting a larger one. The moon is Earth's natural satellite. There are also many artificial satellites orbiting Earth, which are used for observation and communication.

Within the space of our solar system are also countless asteroids—chunks of rock or metal that range in size from small planets to grains of sand. The heaviest concentration is the asteroid belt, where thousands orbit the sun between Jupiter and Mars. Sometimes asteroids enter the Earth's atmosphere. We call these meteors.

Our solar system is also host to comets—chunks of rock, ice, and gas—that pass through our space. Occasionally we can see their telltale vapor tail. The best-known of these is Haley's Comet, which passes into our view every 76 years. Its next sighting should occur in 2061.

Name: _____ **Date:** _____

I have an unusual pet and an unusual problem. Chamile is my pet chameleon. I have a big glass tank set up for her with lots of plants, rocks, and a little pond. I regularly provide insects, which she catches by shooting out her sticky tongue. It is so funny to watch her. Each of her bulgy eyes moves separately, and when she spots a meal, even clear across the cage, she's caught it and rolled her long tongue back in with it faster than I can see. She's a great pet and has a luxury terrarium for a home. The problem is she seems to prefer my room.

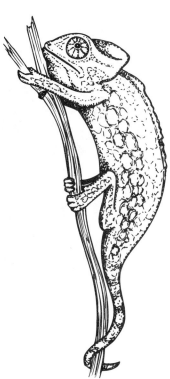

When she is in the tank among the leaves, she is very difficult to spot. That wouldn't be so bad except that she takes every opportunity to escape into my room. You would think it would be easy to spot a bright green lizard among my things. But, chameleons are masters of camouflage. Unlike other animals that are brown to blend in with sticks or speckled to blend in with sand, Chamile can at will change to blend in with whatever is around her, including my curtains, rug, and bedspread. Eventually she comes back to her home in the terrarium, but I worry that she may be out and about and I will sit on her or something!

To solve this problem I consulted a book about lizards. I found something that just might work the next time she decides to hide by changing her colors. I read that chameleons react to changes in light and, if angry, they turn black! Perhaps if I shine a bright flashlight around the room and catch her unprepared, she will show herself.

O True   O False   1. A chameleon is a type of amphibian.

O True   O False   2. Chameleons can move their eyes independently.

O True   O False   3. Chameleons are the only animals that use camouflage to hide.

O True   O False   4. Chamile's owner provides live food for her.

O True   O False   5. The proper cage for a chameleon is an aquarium.

O True   O False   6. If angered, a chameleon may turn bright red.

O True   O False   7. Chameleons can change color by choice.

O True   O False   8. Chameleons are brown to blend in with sticks.

O True   O False   9. A chameleon catches its prey with its sticky tongue.

O True   O False   10. Chamile's owner knows the flashlight plan will solve the problem.

Name: _____   **Date:** _____

Directions: *Read the story. Look for details. Then write TRUE or FALSE under each statement.*

Fashion and Function

The ancient Chinese are responsible for the invention of many objects and items that we commonly use today. The umbrella is one of these items.

The first umbrellas appeared about 1,600 years ago. They were constructed with oiled paper, rice paper, glue, and bamboo. The outsides of the umbrellas were often decorated with colorful paintings of flowers, birds, and other intricate designs. However, these fragile paper umbrellas were not used to shield a person from rain. Women in the Qing dynasty used them to protect their skin from the sun. Umbrellas and parasols became very fashionable for both men and women and were viewed as a symbol of high rank in ancient Chinese society.

1. The Chinese invented the umbrella about 1,600 years ago.

_____

2. Ancient Chinese umbrellas were used as protection from rain.

_____

3. The ancient Chinese were responsible for inventing many items still used today.

_____

4. Rice and oiled papers were used to make the first umbrellas.

_____

5. Men did not use umbrellas.

_____

6. Only Chinese peasants used umbrellas.

_____

7. Early umbrellas were often decorated with bright colors and pictures.

_____

8. Umbrellas were symbols of high society rank.

_____

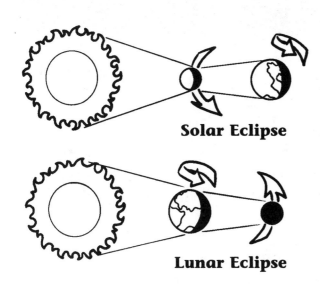

Solar Eclipse

Lunar Eclipse

Eclipses

When either the Earth or the moon blocks the light of the sun, we experience the phenomenon called an eclipse. An eclipse is the shadow cast by the Earth or the moon, blocking the light of the sun.

During a solar eclipse, the moon passes between the sun and the Earth. Its shadow is cast on the Earth's surface. When the Earth passes between the sun and the moon we experience a lunar eclipse. In the event of a lunar eclipse, the Earth's shadow is cast on the face of the moon.

Before science could provide answers, people were frightened of eclipses and thought them to be bad omens. However, we now know that solar and lunar eclipses are normal and predictable events that occur many times a year.

1. An eclipse is a shadow cast by the Earth or the moon.

_____

2. A solar eclipse happens when the Earth passes between the sun and the moon.

_____

3. In the event of a lunar eclipse, the Earth's shadow passes over the face of the sun.

_____

4. People were once frightened of eclipses.

_____

5. Eclipses are bad luck.

_____

6. Eclipses happen only once every ten years.

_____

7. Eclipses are normal and predictable events.

_____

Name: _____   **Date:** _____

Directions: *Below are excerpts from different stories. Decide if the story is being told by a character in the story or told by an outside narrator.*

1. ....I went over to the trough for some feed. Goose teased me as usual. I went to my friends in the stalls. "She's relentless... and mean!" I complained. They listened (or seemed to) and...

_____

2. ...She left the room with her head hung low. Sighing, she whispered under her breath, "I'm going to have to get some help with social studies. I'm just not getting it."....

_____

3. ...The men had been at sea for months. They were tired and thin from poor diet. Their clothes were tattered and their skin burned. Perhaps today land would be sighted...

_____

4. ...When Tanya got home from school there was a huge box on the front step. She was very curious about what could be inside, but dared not open it because it was addressed to her older brother, Jared. She couldn't wait until he got home to find out....

_____

5. ...As soon as the garage door shut and the humans pulled away, we started to chase around. I had always had my eye on those curtains and took my chance to climb them. Myrtle jumped on top of the TV, a place we are forbidden to sit on....

_____

6. ..."May I stay over and eat at Ian's?" asked Sean. "If Mrs. Lewis invited you," answered Mom. "But be home by eight." There was silence on the other end of the phone. "Sean?" Mom asked. "Never mind, Mom," said Sean. "I just found out they're having tuna casserole, and I'll be coming home for dinner." Mom smiled. "So are we," she said to herself....

_____

Directions: *An author has a purpose in mind for writing. Some styles are stronger than others for certain purposes. Read the explanations below. Then identify from which point of view each passage was written.*

first person
The focus is on the <u>writer</u>. Uses words such as I, me, us and we.

second person
The focus is on the <u>reader</u>. Uses words such as you and your.

third person
The focus is on the <u>subject</u>. Uses words such as it, they, them, he, she, as well as names.

1. If you plan to go to college, it is a good idea to start thinking about it early in high school. Besides keeping good grades, you can increase your chances of getting into the college of your choice by being involved in extra-curricular activities and community programs.

   This is written in the _____ person.

2. The unicorn is a mythical creature described in ancient Greek and Roman stories. It is like a horse but has a single spiral horn.

   This is written in the _____ person.

3. If you are ever in Southern California, you will want to visit the Wild Animal Park just outside San Diego. This is one of the few places in which animals are free to roam large areas that are like their natural environment. From the tram you can see rhinos grazing and gazelles running.

   This is written in the _____ person.

4. This may sound strange, but one of my favorite things to do is to iron clothes. I find it relaxing. It is something that lets me spend time thinking and daydreaming while still accomplishing something.

   This is written in the _____ person.

5. When you drink through a straw, a partial vacuum is formed. Liquid from the drink rises to fill the space and reach your mouth.

   This is written in the _____ person.

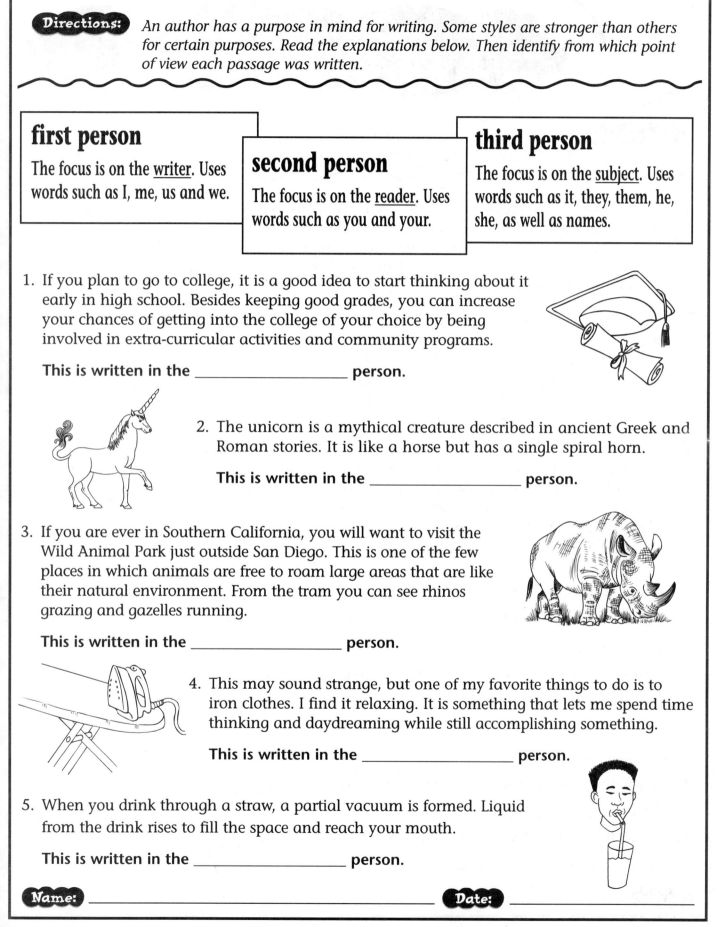

Name: _____   **Date:** _____

> If ten people all see the same thing, there will be ten different accounts of it. That's because each has a unique point of view. It's the same with story characters.

Directions: *Below is the same story about the annual Dale family camping trip told from three different points of view. Read each and answer the questions.*

A. We look forward to these outings because it allows us to relax away from work and spend time with the whole family. Since we both have office jobs, we especially appreciate the natural environment and the "downtime" of trudging through the woods and sleeping in the open air.

B. Every year we take a family camping trip. I really enjoy these trips because it gives me a chance to forget about school and just hang out in nature. There's nothing like building a fire and cooking fresh fish I caught myself in the lake. My idea of fun is sleeping under the stars with no sound but the rustling of wildlife in the bushes.

C. Yuck! Another camping trip. Even though I am older now, I am still too young to do any of the stuff that would be fun. Mostly Mom and Dad are telling me what I can't do—climb the trees, pick up snakes or lizards I find, or throw stones. Night is the worst. I have to share a tent with my big brother and he purposely tells me stuff that scares me.

1. Which description did Tim Dale, age 13, write? _____ Tom, age 8? _____

2. From Mr. and Mrs. Dale's point of view, what are the two main advantages of the annual camping trip? _____

3. From Tom's point of view, he's not allowed to do anything fun. What do you think his parents' perspective on these activities is? _____

4. Do you think Tim purposely tries to scare Tom? If so, why? If not, why does Tom think so?

   _____

5. Do you think Tom's view of the camping trips will change in five years? If so, how? If not, why not? _____

6. Do you think Mr. and Mrs. Dale know how their sons feel about camping? Why or why not?

   _____

Name: _____ **Date:** _____

The Trouble With Valerie by Maxheimer

My owner, Valerie, just doesn't get it. Sure, she pets me when she gets home from school, but then she goes off and does homework or to her friends' without me. Doesn't she understand that I am supposed to be her best friend? And here's another thing. She comes and goes as she pleases, but I am stuck in the house all day by myself. She should get me a playmate or at least a doggie door so I can go out in the yard. There's more. When I bark, she shushes me. I am only trying to express myself! And what's with this leash business? Doesn't she trust me? Finally, the supreme insult—a bath. Fleas or no fleas, you don't see cats having to endure such humiliation. I do love Valerie, but she treats me like a dog!

1. From Maxheimer's point of view, what two things should Valerie get for him?

   _____   _____

2. What is Maxheimer's *main* complaint about Valerie? _____

   _____

3. What is Maxheimer's explanation of barking? _____

4. What does Maxheimer imply he would do if he were not subjected to being on a leash?

   _____

5. Does Maxheimer enjoy having Valerie give him a bath? _____

6. Does Maxheimer feel that cats have it better or worse than dogs? _____

7. How does Maxheimer feel about being treated "like a dog"? _____

My Dog Maxheimer by Valerie

_____

_____

_____

_____

_____

_____

_____

_____

Name: _____   **Date:** _____

Directions: *Can you identify an animal just by looking at its feet? Here's your chance. But beware. The Word Box has the animal names you need, but also some you don't!*

Word Box

dog   alligator   cat   chicken   rabbit   frog   person   hawk   lizard
bear   elephant   chameleon   ostrich   deer   duck   horse   monkey

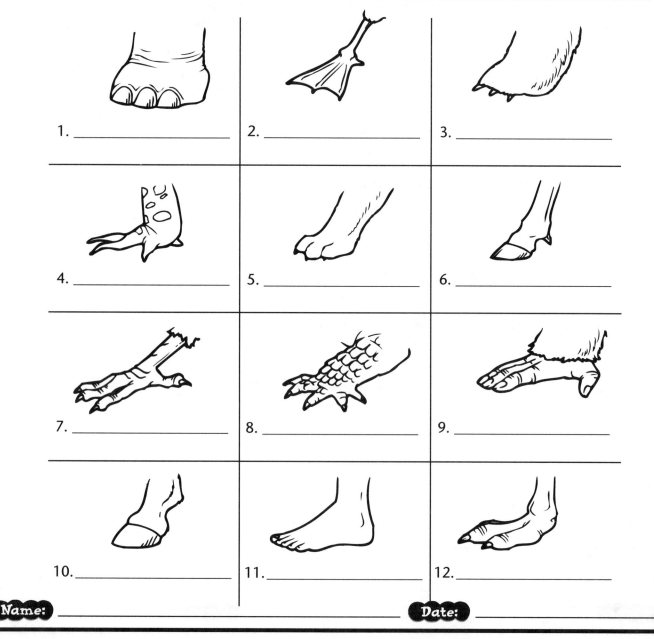

1. _____

2. _____

3. _____

4. _____

5. _____

6. _____

7. _____

8. _____

9. _____

10. _____

11. _____

12. _____

Name: _____   Date: _____

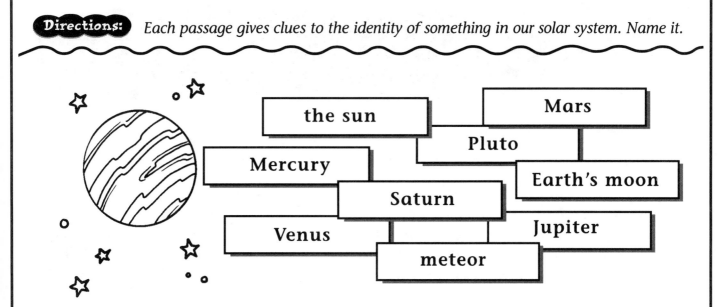

the sun

Mars

Pluto

Mercury

Earth's moon

Saturn

Venus

Jupiter

meteor

1. Has mountains, canyons, volcanoes, and even seasons. Known as the red planet because of the dusty surface soil is filled with iron oxide (rust).

_____

2. Debris from space that's entered Earth's atmosphere. Heat from friction causes it to glow. As it moves, it is seen as a streak of light—but it is NOT a star, shooting or otherwise.

_____

3. The star nearest Earth (93 million miles) and the only star in our solar system. Medium-sized as stars go.

_____

4. Known for its red spot and swirling colors, it is the largest planet in the solar system. It has 16 moons and no solid surface.

_____

5. Smaller than Earth's moon, it has a long and lopsided orbit. Sometimes it is closer to the sun than Neptune and other times further.

_____

6. Called the "morning star" but actually a planet about the size of Earth. Covered in a thick blanket of yellow clouds containing deadly sulfuric acid.

_____

7. Orbits Earth only 239,000 miles away. Has no atmosphere. Its gravity (1/5 of Earth's) causes the ocean tides.

_____

8. When Galileo first observed it in 1610, he called its rings "ears." They are really more than 1,000 bands of rock and ice orbiting this planet.

_____

Name: _____   **Date:** _____

Directions: *Read the story. Then, place the statements in the order they happened by numbering 1–7.*

Captain James Cook

Captain James Cook is considered one of the greatest explorers the world has ever known. He was born in Yorkshire, England, in 1728, and died in the Sandwich Islands (now known as the Hawaiian Islands) in 1779.

Cook led many voyages of exploration on his ship, the Endeavour, on behalf of the British Empire. He was hailed as an excellent navigator and a respected captain. He also was the first captain to prevent his crew from developing scurvy, a disease that occurs from a lack of Vitamin C. He did this by insisting they eat fresh fruit and pickled cabbage.

Cook was the first European to visit the Pacific Islands and is said to have sailed farther south than any other explorer in European history. Cook and his crew visited many lands, including Australia and New Zealand, and claimed them as British territory.

_____ James Cook died in the Sandwich Islands.

_____ James Cook was born in 1728.

_____ Cook was the first European to visit the Pacific Islands.

_____ Cook insisted his crew eat fresh fruit and pickled cabbage.

_____ Cook claimed Australia and New Zealand as British territories.

_____ Cook prevented his crew from developing scurvy, a disease caused by a lack of Vitamin C.

_____ Cook led many voyages on behalf of the British Empire.

Name: _____   Date: _____

Chocolate

The cacao tree of Central and South America is responsible for giving us the main ingredient in one of the world's favorite treats—chocolate. The cacao tree produces pods that, when split open, reveal seeds and pulp. The mass is removed and left to ferment and dry. Then the seeds, known as cacao beans, are separated out, cleaned, roasted, and ground. In the process of grinding, cocoa butter is released and the mixture forms a liquid called chocolate liquor. Hardened bars are made by squeezing out the liquid. Raw chocolate is bitter in taste.

The Aztecs of Central America were the first to make a drink from cacao, spices, and peppers. Later, the Spanish explorers of the early 16th century revised this recipe by removing the peppers and spices and adding sugar to the drink instead. Over a hundred years later, a Frenchman created blocks of chocolate that soon became a much-loved sweet treat that is still enjoyed by many to this day.

____ Bars are hardened by squeezing out the liquid.

____ Chocolate liquor is created.

____ The mass is removed, fermented, and dried.

____ Beans are separated, cleaned, roasted, and ground.

____ Pods split open and reveal the seeds and pulp.

1. Q: _____

   A: The Aztecs were the first to make a drink from cacao beans.

2. Q: _____

   A: The Spanish may have substituted sugar in their chocolate drink because they did not like the spicy flavor of the original Aztec recipe.

3. Q: _____

   A: The first chocolate blocks were created in the 17th century.

Name: _____ **Date:** _____

A Day in the Life of Aaron

Imagine this graph showing one typical school day in Aaron's life. You are going to fill in how he spends his time. First study the blank graph. How much time does each section represent? Read about Aaron's day. Then follow the directions below.

Aaron gets up early to do his paper route. It takes about two hours. He returns home about 8:00 and has breakfast, then walks the half-hour to school at 8:30. He is in school from 9:00 to 3:00. At 3:30, he's back home. He likes to get most of his homework over with right away, so he studies from 3:30 to 5:00. From 5:00 to 6:00, he relaxes by watching TV or riding his bike over to Jeff's. Aaron's family has dinner from 6:00 to 6:30. After dinner Aaron does the dishes and other chores until about 7:30. From 7:30 to 8:30, he's free to do whatever he wants. Sometimes he plays computer games with his brother, sometimes he reads or works on his model building. At 8:30, he puts in another half-hour of studying. Finally, he reads until he falls asleep around 10:00. Then, it's up again at 6:00 to deliver papers.

Put Aaron's day in order using 1–8. Then, calculate the total time for each activity. Use colored pencils or markers to color the graph:

___ homework/studying/reading (RED) _____	___ in bed asleep (PURPLE) _____
___ in school (YELLOW) _____	___ relaxing or free time (GREEN) _____
___ eating breakfast & dinner (BLUE) _____	___ traveling to/from school (BLACK) _____
___ doing chores (BROWN) _____	___ paper route (ORANGE) _____

Name: _____ **Date:** _____

Have you ever noticed that music has mood? It can be happy, sad, serious, or silly. Stories have mood, too. The author sets the tone for the story.

Directions: *Read each story excerpt. Highlight or underline any words you feel set the tone for the story. Then choose the word that best describes the overall mood.*

1. Joanna sat cross-legged on her bed, hugging her pillow, her head hung low. Mom walked by her door, noticed her just sitting there, and stopped. "What's wrong?" she asked. "Didn't you get any classes with Carla?" Joanna sighed. "Yeah, I did, but Carla told me today she's moving in two months."

   The overall mood is (check one) ☐ happy ☐ sad ☐ serious ☐ silly

2. Jim came home from school walking on air. His older brother saw him and said, "What's up with you?" Jim suppressed his smile, then said, "Oh nothing. I just won first place in the science fair, that's all. They are sending me and my project to the state finals."

   Is time travel possible?

   $E=MC^2$

   The overall mood is (check one) ☐ happy ☐ sad ☐ serious ☐ silly

3. Dr. Jensen looked at the X ray of Brownie's leg. He pursed his lips and knitted his brow. Brownie lay on the table wrapped in a towel. She was breathing but otherwise still. Dr. Jensen gently touched the little dog's head. "Well, Miss Brownie, you have fractured a bone in your leg." Then turning to me, "Brownie will need surgery to repair this, son."

   ☐ ☐ ☐ ☐

   The overall mood is (check one)   happy   sad   serious   silly

4. Halloween was coming and Shandra was in the store looking at costumes for her little sister. Shandra would be staying home to greet trick-or-treaters but that didn't mean she couldn't have a little fun. On the wall was a section of costumes for pets. She spotted just the one for her dachshund, Derry—a hotdog costume! She giggled and bought it.

   The overall mood is (check one) ☐ happy ☐ sad ☐ serious ☐ silly

Name: _____   **Date:** _____

Every day on my way home from school I pass old Mrs. Victor's house. It has looked the same for as long as I can remember. Someone once said it was even older than Mrs. Victor herself, and she must be about a hundred.

I often wonder about Mrs. Victor and that run-down house. They seem so much alike that they are almost one thing. I have seen her a few times—walking slowly up the path with her rolling pull-cart containing just one bag of groceries. The walkway that leads to the house is stone but full of cracks—not unlike Mrs. Victor's face. The wood sides of the house are buckling and weathered, as is Mrs. Victor's skin. And what is inside? A lonely empty place where no one comes to visit. Yet, there they are—Mrs. Victor and her house—each a living relic in a modern world.

This morning as I passed by, I saw old Mrs. Victor through the sheer curtains behind which she leads her veiled life. She was sitting in a chair, perhaps knitting, perhaps doing nothing at all. She happened to look up and saw me walking by but didn't really notice me. Am I just another part of a world she feels left out of? A person moving through time who has left her behind? I felt a pang of sadness for her and right then decided to do something about it.

My friend Kerry's cat had kittens a few weeks ago, and he's been looking for homes for them. After school, I stopped by and asked to "borrow" two of them. I took them home, fixed up a basket with a big bow, and went to Mrs. Victor's.

As I rang her bell, I wondered if I was being presumptuous. Perhaps we would not be welcome. But, to my delight, when she opened the door and saw us, her pallid face positively turned to glowing. She accepted my gift and new life seemed to pour into not only Mrs. Victor, but her house as well.

1. Describe the mood of the story. _____

2. Underline four or more words/phrases that set the tone of the story.

3. What does the author mean by a *living relic*? _____

    a veiled life? _____

4. In what ways does the author compare Mrs. Victor to her house? _____

    _____

5. Why did the author ask to "borrow" the kittens instead of just saying he'd found them a

    home? _____

6. Read the last sentence again. Life cannot actually *pour*. Which kind of expression is this: a

    simile or a metaphor? _____

7. What shift in mood does the author create from the beginning to the end of the story?

    _____

Directions: *The story below is based on the life of Naturalist Louis Agassiz. Follow the plot to see how an imaginative young boy turns into a Harvard professor. Then summarize the plot. Describe the events that mark the stages in the life of Louis Agassiz.*

It was a warm evening in Switzerland in 1814. Company was coming to visit the Agassiz family. Seven-year-old Louis wanted to help entertain the guests, so he offered to show them his pets. And little Louis had quite a few to show. He sent his little brother, Augustine, to bring down the "householders" while he, Louis, showed the guests his "chorusers" out on the porch. When they came back in from looking at all the birds, the parlor was covered with turtles—big ones, little ones, brown ones, green ones. As they all scrambled to gather up the wayward reptiles, one guest asked Louis why he called turtles householders. "Because they hold their own houses!" Louis beamed.

As Louis grew up, he continued to collect and study all sorts of creatures. In 1846 he moved to the United States and later became a professor at Harvard University teaching classes in nature study. He was well known and respected for his vast knowledge. One April Fool's Day a student tried to trick the professor. He took various parts of different insects, meticulously glued them together, then presented it to Agassiz asking him to identify the fancy bug. The professor gave it a serious look, then quickly pronounced, "Why, yes, this is definitely a humbug."

SETTING: _____

MAIN CHARACTER(s): _____

Event #1 (Louis as a child) _____

_____

Result: _____

Event #2 (when Louis grew up) _____

_____

Result: _____

Event #3 (Louis as a professor) _____

_____

Result: _____

Name: _____ **Date:** _____

O.T. Sander was born Oliver Thomas Sander. The O.T. came later and if you were to think that O.T. stands for Oliver Thomas, you'd be wrong.

Oliver Thomas was due to be born on September 21, but his mamma and papa knew babies rarely come exactly on the day they are predicted to come. So, on September 21, they weren't ready, but Oliver Thomas came as scheduled. Papa hurried up and got the nursery ready, and when Oliver Thomas came home from the hospital right on time, his room was ready.

Mama and Papa Sander were attentive parents. They knew new babies needed to be fed on a schedule. They agreed to take turns for the 2:00 am feeding. The first night, they were both so tired, they would've slept right through it, but Oliver Thomas woke them up screaming at precisely 2:00 am that night and every night for the next few weeks.

And so it went that Oliver Thomas grew to be a big, healthy boy. He ate breakfast at 8:00, lunch at noon, and dinner at 6:00. He brushed his teeth (after he got some) at 7:30, took a bath at 7:40, listened to Mama or Papa read a story, then fell asleep at 8:15.

The night before he started kindergarten, Mama told him it was important to be on time. Oliver Thomas walked into class at exactly 9:00 am and, at 11:29 he got ready to go home—every single day. If the teacher said he could use the paint table for 15 minutes, that's what Oliver Thomas did.

Throughout first grade, the other kids would keep looking on the back wall at the clock (the ones who could tell time and even the ones who couldn't) to see what time it was (and how long until lunch or recess). Oliver Thomas never looked at the clock. He just knew. By the end of first grade, or maybe even sooner, some people started calling him O.T. It stuck.

1. The first paragraph gives you a hint about what the goal of the story is. What is it?

_____

2. The author never tells you what O.T. stands for but gives you lots of clues. What did you

conclude it stands for? _____

3. What was the very first thing Oliver Thomas did to earn his nickname? _____

_____

4. Find and write at least four words from the story that have something to do with time.

_____

5. Are you more like Oliver Thomas or unlike him, and why? _____

_____

Sometimes reading takes a little detective work. Look for clues that tell you if the author wrote it to inform you or persuade you.

Directions: *Read each sentence below. Think about its purpose. Is it to give factual information, or is it someone's opinion? First, underline any words that signal that it is an opinion. Then copy only the sentences that are written for the purpose of informing.*

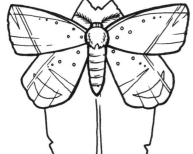

- You should read at least one book per week.

- In some places houses are built on stilts.

- Mars is sometimes called the Red Planet.

- It is important to recycle cans and newspapers.

- Climate is the weather over a long period of time.

- Things that cost more are better.

- The U.S. government has a system of checks and balances.

- It is hard to get into a good college.

- Roses are the prettiest flowers.

- All living things need water to thrive.

- Riding a bike is faster than skateboarding.

- There are distinct differences between butterflies and moths.

1. _____

2. _____

3. _____

4. _____

_____

5. _____

6. _____

_____

Name: _____ **Date:** _____

1. When you think of the Arctic, do you picture everyone living in igloos? Long ago the Inuit built igloos as their winter homes. They were very clever builders. Today, people do not live in igloos as homes but may construct them for temporary shelter as needed.

   The sentence crossed out does not belong in this paragraph because _____ _____ _____

2. People who live in hot, dry desert climates often build homes with thick walls. Adobe is pretty and practical. The thick walls are effective for two reasons. They keep the home cool during the hot days, but also, when the temperature drops at night, the thick walls keep the heat trapped inside.

   The sentence crossed out does not belong in this paragraph because _____ _____ _____

3. Nomads are people who live by traveling from one place to another. They set up temporary homes, such as tents or huts, where they stay for awhile, then move to another area. They also have animals. Nomads may stay in one place for a season or just a few days.

   The sentence crossed out does not belong in this paragraph because _____ _____ _____

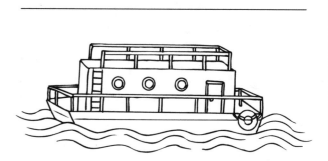

4. Some people live on floating homes, or houseboats. Though often not spacious, houseboats can have all the amenities of houses on land—electricity, showers, kitchens, and even computers. It would be fun to live on a houseboat.

   The sentence crossed out does not belong in this paragraph because _____ _____ _____

Name: _____

Date: _____

1. You should vote for Jackie in the upcoming student representative election. She is the best choice because she knows how every seventh-grade student thinks and will represent each one of us. She is a good listener and a good student. She knows what your concerns are and will fight to make our school better.

What is this trying to persuade you to do? _____

What exaggerated claim is made about Jackie? _____

_____

What specific qualifications are given as reasons to vote for Jackie? _____

_____

Would you vote for Jackie? Why or why not? _____

_____

2. Wouldn't you like all your friends to envy you? Then you need to have the best and fastest sport shoes available—**Lightnings**! Don't settle for less. Look for the **Lightning** logo, or don't look at all! Only $69.95 a pair.

What is this trying to persuade you to do?

_____

How does this appeal to your emotions or feelings?

_____

How does it guide you away from buying a similar product made by someone else?

_____

What exaggerated claim is made, hoping you'll believe it? _____

_____

Who would buy these shoes, and why? _____

_____

emotional appeal

(the product will make you look, feel, or be better; it will provide something you think you need or lack) **Example:** a computer that improves your grades.

_____
_____
_____
_____
_____
_____

_____
_____
_____
_____
_____

endorsement

(a famous person says the product is the one you should buy) **Example:** a movie star telling you what shampoo to use.

bait or hook

(something is offered free or extra if you buy the main product) **Example:** buy one shirt at full price and get a second pair free.

_____
_____
_____
_____
_____
_____

_____
_____
_____
_____
_____

exaggerated claim

(the product is claimed to do more than it does) **Example:** a diet supplement that guarantees that you will lose 10 pounds in 2 days.

Name: _____ **Date:** _____

You're not expected to remember every detail of what you read—just the essentials. That's why summarizing is such a useful reading tool. Do you use it?

Directions: *A good summary is short and contains general information about the story rather than lots of specifics. Read the summary of the classic fable of "The Boy Who Cried Wolf." Then follow the format to write a summary of another fable you know.*

title The Boy Who Cried Wolf

setting A boy was left alone to tend sheep high on a hill above the town. He was told that if a wolf should come by to cry "WOLF" and the townspeople would come to his aid.

problem The boy became bored, and though no wolf had come, he cried "WOLF" and the townspeople came running.

climax After doing this several times, when a wolf really did appear, the townspeople did not believe him and did not come.

resolution The boy learned that a liar is not to be believed, even when he tells the truth.

title _____

setting _____
_____
_____

problem _____
_____

climax _____
_____

resolution _____
_____

Name: _____ **Date:** _____

Directions: *Summarize the plot of a movie you have seen and a book you have read. For each, first list the title. Then in paragraph form, briefly give the setting, main characters, the problem, key events, and resolution.*

movie summary

____

book summary

____

Name: ______________________ **Date:** ______________

Want to have some fun recalling story events? Try mapping, which is simply presenting information in a visual form.

Directions: *Below is a mixed-up list of events from the classic fairy tale* Little Red Riding Hood. *Fill in the events in order on the map, beginning at Red Riding Hood and ending at Grandmother's house.*

- The wolf disguises himself as Grandma and waits for Red Riding Hood.
- The wolf identifies himself and his real intentions.
- Red Riding Hood enters the forest carrying a basket of goodies for Grandma.

- A wolf sees Red Riding Hood and goes off ahead to Grandma's.
- Red Riding Hood comments how strange Grandma is looking and speaking.
- A hunter comes by and rescues her.

The first automobile race was held in 1895 in Chicago. There were six cars in the race, powered by gasoline or electricity. A gasoline-powered model won by going 54 miles in an amazing 7½ hours.

Though Henry Ford had built a gasoline-powered buggy three years before back in Michigan, he was unable to attend the race for lack of funds. Still, Ford believed the future was in cars. He began work on a factory that would produce cars fast and cheap. People thought his ideas about assembly-line production were crazy.

It took Henry Ford eight years to build the now-famous Model T. (Ford labeled his models after the alphabet to show progress. Nineteen other models—A through S—preceded the T.)

In 1908, when Henry Ford started production on the Model T, he aspired to rolling off the assembly line a car a minute. Six years later, the millionth Model T came off the assembly line one minute after the previous one.

Fifteen million Model T's had been built before it was taken out of production in 1927. The Model T was the first affordable automobile Although very successful, people were starting to demand fancier models. It was at this time, also, that other automobile companies were coming out with speedier, better-looking cars.

Name: _____   Date: _____

Reading Comprehension • Saddleback Publishing, Inc. ©2002   130   3 Watson, Irvine, CA 92618•Phone (888)SDL-BACK•www.sdlback.com

Long ago, there lived a young woman in Greece whose name was Arachne. There was nothing she loved more than spinning and weaving at her loom, making the finest of cloths. People admired her work and came from near and far to praise it. Arachne herself thought there could be no other person in all the world who could spin as fine as she.

When asked if she had been taught by the gods, Arachne responded that she alone had a gift and perhaps she could teach them!

By and by, a woman came to see Arachne. She was Athena, queen of the air, and had heard of her boasting. When Athena asked Arachne directly who had taught her to spin, Arachne boldly stuck to her story. Athena, annoyed by Arachne's audacity, challenged her to a spinning contest in which Jupiter would be the judge. Arachne agreed.

When the contest commenced, Arachne sat in her garden among the flowers and insects. Athena sat in the sky. Arachne spun beautiful webbed patterns and the gods were in awe. Then Athena began to spin. She used the gold of the sunlight, the fleece of the clouds, the deep green of the moss, and the blue of the sky. At once Jupiter declared Athena the winner, and Arachne was banned from ever using a loom again.

But, Athena felt pity for the girl. She touched her with a magic needle, and at once she was turned into a spider. She was left in the garden to spin to her heart's content.

It is said that she remains there still, spinning and weaving marvelous webs. Perhaps you have seen her yourself.

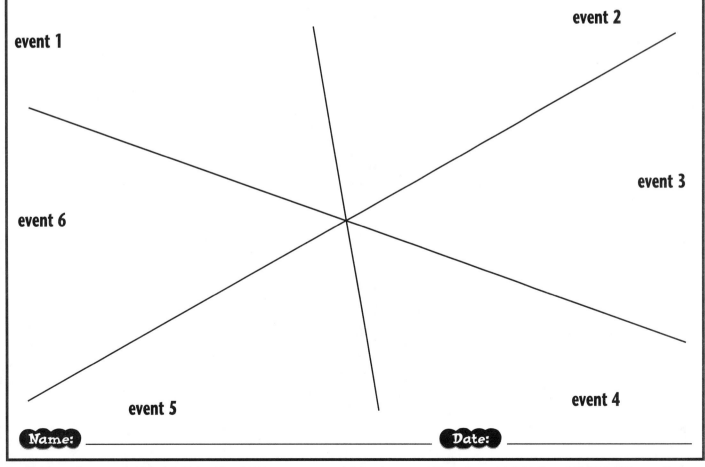

event 1

event 2

event 3

event 6

event 5

event 4

The firemen rested on their cots
Some playing cards, some napping.
When suddenly the siren blew!
Something big was happening.

Within a minute every man
Had jumped up with a jolt.
They hastily put on their gear
And to the truck did bolt.

The engine sped forth to the scene
Men hanging on the sides.
Blaring out their warning sound
For all to let them by.

The truck arrived in lightning time.
The smoke was pouring out.
And from the third floor window
Mac heard a young boy shout.

The ladder went up quickly
As he climbed he felt the heat.
Mac reached the boy and heard the cheers
From crowds down in the street.

In just a few more minutes
The building was secure.
Of these brave men and women
Who could ask for more?

Name: _____

Date: _____

Who

What

Where

When

Why

Mapping is not just for story elements or plot. Mapping is also a fun way to compare or show information about characters.

Directions: Use a story you have read recently or know well that has two main characters. Compare the characters by completing the maps below.

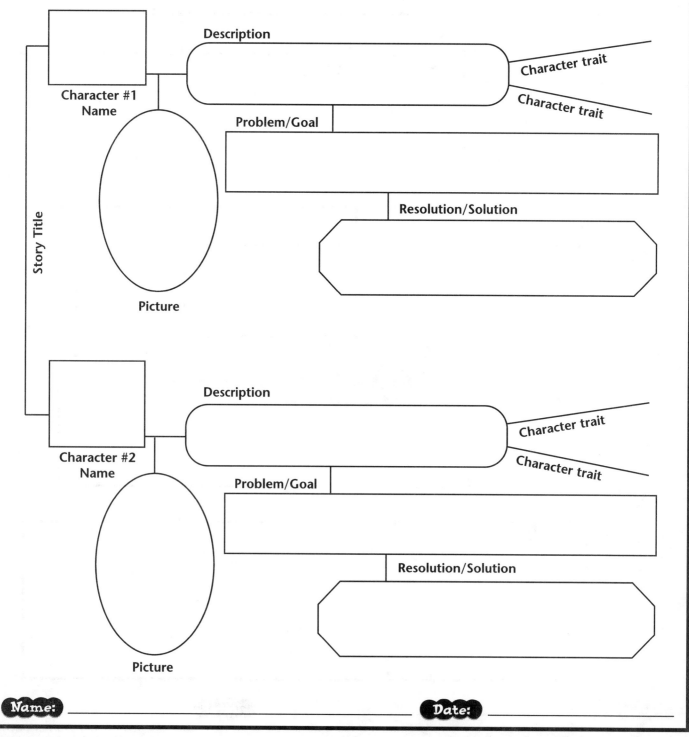

Story Title

Character #1 Name

Description

Character trait

Character trait

Picture

Problem/Goal

Resolution/Solution

Character #2 Name

Description

Character trait

Character trait

Picture

Problem/Goal

Resolution/Solution

- was a First Lady
- lived from 1884-1962
- was shy and awkward as a youth
- was raised a Quaker
- lived from 1768-1849
- known for her social graces
- saved important documents when British invaded Washington

- among the most admired women of her time
- placed high priority on fine fashion
- was sensitive to underprivileged
- was devoted to her husband, the President
- presided at the first inaugural ball
- was a prolific writer—magazines and books
- served as chair of the UN Human Rights Commission

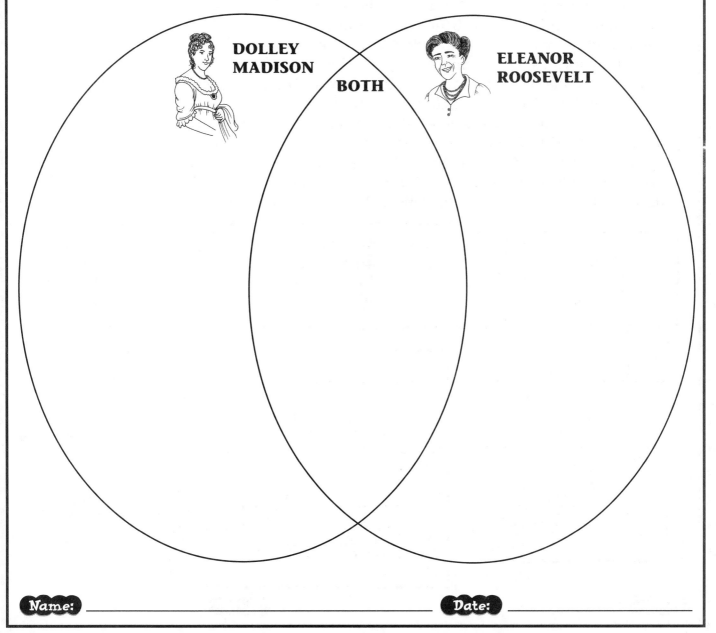

DOLLEY MADISON   BOTH   ELEANOR ROOSEVELT

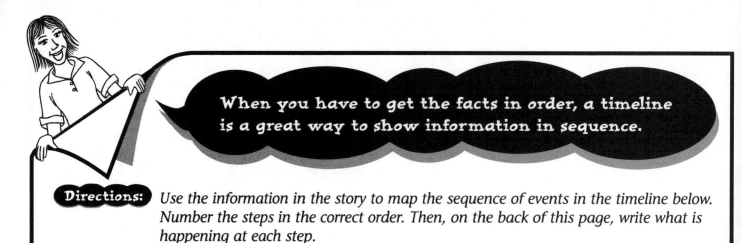

When you have to get the facts in order, a timeline is a great way to show information in sequence.

Directions: *Use the information in the story to map the sequence of events in the timeline below. Number the steps in the correct order. Then, on the back of this page, write what is happening at each step.*

Mr. Gerrard owns a business that sells auto parts. He buys the parts he stocks from many different manufacturers, then sells them to repair shops and individuals. He must be very organized to keep track of all the different parts he buys and sells.

To ensure that his customers are happy and he does not lose money, Mr. Gerrard follows specific procedures. The typical order takes about $\frac{1}{2}$ hour to process. At 9:00 am Mr. G. checks his mail (regular and e-mail). He takes about 5 minutes to sort it into three types: orders, bills and other business, and personal. He gives the order to Mr. Tanner to enter the orders into the computer. About 5 minutes later, Mr. T. prints a "pick sheet" and gives it to Ms. Windly, who "picks" the products off the shelves in the warehouse for shipping. This takes about 9 minutes. Mrs. W. gives the pick list and products to Mr. Hebner, who quickly rechecks that the right products have been picked. If so, he boxes them and labels them for shipping. Within 10 minutes, Mr. H. sends the pick sheet back to Mr. T., noting if all items were shipped or if any were out of stock. Mr. T. takes 5 minutes to adjust the invoice to match the shipment and enter the updated information in the computer. If there are backorders, Mr. T. lets Mr. Gerrard know so that he can order those items from the manufacturer. By 9:30 the customer's order and invoice are sent.

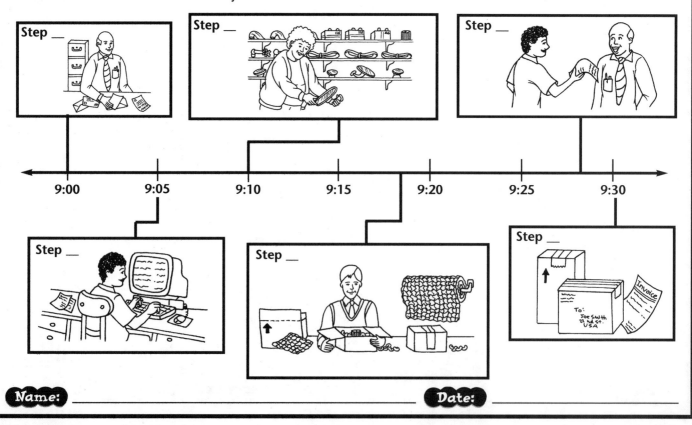

Scope & Sequence

Students	word analysis	prefixes/suffixes	following directions	visual/context clues	vocabulary	signal words	dictionary	practicing life-skills reading	idioms/similes/metaphors	five W's	analogies	classification	recognizing time elements	questioning techniques	prediction	inferences	graphic devices	main idea	outlining	summarize

Scope & Sequence

Students	generalizations	graphic devices	trivial/redundant information	story genre	topic/supporting sentences	compare/contrast	cause/effect	character analysis	perspective analysis	determining fact/opinion	factual recall	author's view/purpose	character's view/purpose	setting analysis	story sequence	mood/tone analysis	plot analysis	read to inform/persuade	plot summary	story mapping

Answer Key

Page 6
1. a. slow; plodded
b. boreal
c. tied
d. avoid
2. a. presume
b. an opinion
c. eating
d. afford
e. Wording will vary.

Page 7
(Must be in this order).
1. pause, paws
2. manner, manor
3. won, one
4. chews, choose
5. feet, feat
6. hire, higher
7. lessen, lesson
8. capitol, capital
9. clothes, close

Page 8
1. to brighten or enlighten.
2. someone who watches.
3. 3. Prove to be false or unbelievable.
4. To please, calm, or make peace.
5. A set of names or system of naming.
6. A structure for transporting water.
7. A reason to move or take action.

Page 9
1. perilous
2. generous
3. jealous
4. glorious
5. suspicious
6. nervous
7. curious
8. furious

Page 10
1. postponement
2. retirement
3. fulfillment
4. encouragement
5. adjournment
6. detriment
7. commitment
8. statement

Page 11
1. able to use both hands with equal skill.

2. to carry or bring in.
3. praise given as a result of an action.
4. able to act independently.
5. One who is new at doing something.
6. To enact into law.
7. To leave or empty out.
8. One that resists; enemy.

Page 12
(Answer order).
Stegosaurus Valley
Compsognathus Cave
Jurassic Meadow
Grassy Clearing
Fossil Swamp
Pteranodon Waterfalls
Iguanadon Ridge
Answers will vary. Dr. Digby: The T-Rex is buried in Grassy Clearing, right where we started.

Page 13
Chart spells YES in red.

Page 14
1. related to ships or sailing
2. rude, insensitive
3. twisted and knotty
4. gut feeling, premonition
5. put into effect
6. a jaylike bird
7. egg-producing
8. small group
9. remarked
10. happy, cheerful
11. fake, artificial
12. natural ability, talent

Page 15
1. grueling
2. litany
3. ultimately
4. toiled
5. razzing
6. donned
7. swelled
8. intermittently
9. crammed
10. scouts
11. fumbling
12. profound

Page 16

Page 17
1. hammer
2. meat
3. married
4. hockey
5. trucker
6. sister

Page 18
1. bikes
2. can't tell
3. basketball
4. the label…
5. by plane
6. lower than expected
7. can't tell
8. delighted
9. a sandwich

Page 19
1. 2
2. 5
3. 1
4. 4
5. 3
6. 6
7. 3
8. 7
9. 6
10. 1
11. 8
12. 4
13. 9
14. 2
15. 1
16. 10
17. 5
18. 7

Page 20
1. invoke
2. insolent
3. augment
4. allocate
5. remedy
6. paragon
7. solitude
8. journal
9. humane
10. frugal
11. gumption
12. covenant
Komodo Dragon

Page 21
1. for a limited time; of modern times
2. of the sea; sailor
3. water pipe; water-powered
4. having an end; final/conclusive

Page 22
1. an opposite idea is coming
2. there's more details to come
3. and opposite idea is coming
4. these ideas are in order
5. an opposite idea is coming
6. there's more details to come
7. these ideas are in order

Page 23
Important Point
a key feature
therefore
the main point
noteworthy
most of all
principally
Comparison
rather
however
yet
like; unlike
but
although
Conclusion
as a result
in summary
in conclusion
remember
consequently
hence

Page 24
1. D
2. F
3. A
4. H
5. B
6. G
7. C
8. E

Page 25

Page 26

Listen, my children, and you shall hear..
He said to his friend, If the British march...
Hang a lantern aloft in the belfry arch...
Of the North Church tower a signal...
And I on the opposite shore will be...
Ready to ride and spread the alarm...
For the country folk to be up and to arm...

Page 27
1. c
2. f
3. h
4. a
5. e
6. d
7. b
8. g

Page 28
1. October
2. Yes
3. 4
4. "The Big River"
5. Young Artist Gallery
6. Police Dept.'s Community Halloween party
7. So school children can attend
8. $35

Page 29
1. 3
2. 1
3. 4
4. 4
5. 2
6. 2
7. 4
8. 4
9. 3
10. 1
Answers will vary.

Page 30
1. no
2. 11 am
3. Seattle, WA, Los Angeles, CA
4. Colorado
5. Florida
6. 7 am
7. later
8. 2 pm

Page 31
1. drives me up the wall
2. head swimming with facts
3. hang out; horse of a different color
4. time to get my feet wet
5. her heart sank
6. got tongue-tied
accept reasonable interpretations.

Page 32
1. metaphor; my room is mess
2. Metaphor; friends were close/alike/inseparable
3. simile; sat still
4. simile; swam well
5. simile; my throat felt scratchy
6. simile; in a very quiet way
7. metaphor; a large amount of homework
8. metaphor; puffy white clouds

Page 33
1. Ambrose Staub
2. Paste
3. St. Louis
4. No one knows for sure
5. Elderly
6. They had weak teeth
7. 1903

Page 34
1. Julius Caesar
2. To track the sun
3. For accuracy
4. We still use it today
5. In England

Page 35
(Specific wording will vary).
1. Who gave one of the most well-known speeches in American history?
2. What speech did he give?
3. When did he give it?
4. Why did he give the speech?
5. Where was the cemetery located?

Page 36
1. Queen Hatshepsut's father
2. King or emperor
3. Ancient paintings
4. 1512-1482? B.C.
5. so she would be remembered as a pharaoh

Page 37
1. mow
2. hive
3. write
4. shell
5. uncle
6. color
7. dune
8. sky
9. horse
10. messy

Page 38

Page 39
1. bakery
2. pharmacy
3. veterinarian
4. department store
5. florist
6. auto parts store
7. optometrist
8. gas station
9. office supply store

Page 40
(accept reasonable responses).
1. Vol. 5-Franklin
2. Vol. 4-desert or Vol.1-animals
3. Vol. 3-Civil War or Vol. 17-U.S. History
4. Vol. 1-Amazon or Vol.2-Brazil
5. Vol. 7-human body
6. Vol. 19-whales

Page 41
(Accept any logical conclusion).
1. sequins; the rest are used to attach clothing
2. round; the rest are types of dances
3. shark; the rest are mammals
4. 2,645; the rest have a 0 in the ten's place
5. cactus; the rest are trees
6. blue; the rest are hair colors
7. adult; the rest are young animals

Page 42
1. entertain
2. persuade
3. summarize
4. instruct
5. inform
6. describe

Page 43
1. past
2. future
3. present
4. present
5. past
6. past

Page 44
Accept any reasonable answers.

Page 45
1. a set of amendments to the Constitution
2. several states had agreed to sign the Constitution only if the Bill of Rights was adopted.
3. 2 years, 3 months
4. ten
5. to guarantee freedoms not specifically addressed in the Constitution
6. The Bill of rights differs because a right can only be repealed through the states. In England Parliament can repeal a right.

Page 46
Answers will vary.

Page 47
1. 30 weeks or 7.5 months
2. 1990
3. 225 years (accept 225-230)
4. in 2002: 1982, in 2003: 1983, in 2004: 1984, in 2005: 1985, in 2006:1986
5. fall/autumn
6. 64
7. 1850 or mid 1800s
8. 120

Page 48
1. a storage area
2. a woman
3. true
4. The meeting was prearranged.
5. Story doesn't say
6. In a new way

Page 49
1. thick; dense
2. no; baffling
3. plenty; bountiful
4. pictures; hieroglyphics
5. yes; influence
6. little; mystery

Page 50
(Wording will vary).
1. daydreaming
2. unexpectedly
3. family trait
4. serious; responsible
5. a long time
6. illogical
7. joyful; elated
8. wasn't important

Page 51
1. Arctic/Arctic foxes; far north
2. Not white/distinguished from other owls
3. Both/diurnal
4. Carnivore/eats animals
5. Yes/weighs 4 pounds and can carry more than its weight

Page 52

Page 53
1. a society of Native Americans
2. make you aware of climb
3. sand/dirt mixture
4. for safety; to prevent strangers from entering
5. They were brought inside.

Page 54
(Drawn and labeled).
1. crutch
2. crown
3. radio
4. canteen
5. apron
6. calculator

Page 55
1. Chapter 2
2. 7-10
3. yes
4. Dias
5. After
6. sailed around the world
7. Pre-1500 to 1700
8. It did not occur until after 1700
9. Social Studies, Geography, or History

Page 56
1. Nile Crocodile
2. By its teeth
3. Africa
4. Meat
5. Reptile
6. Yes
7. No
8. Yes
9. Yes

Page 57
1. graph
2. Colorado
3. Congo
4. Longer
5. Volga
6. Volga and Mississippi;

Amazon and Nile
7. Amazon and Nile
8. yes
9. yes
10. no
11. no
12. yes

Page 58
Main idea: though Morse is considered...
1. Yes
2. No
3. No
4. Yes
5. Yes
6. No
7. Yes
8. No

Page 59
1. to bite and chew food; the first step in digestion
2. incisors, canines, molars
3. Front teeth are sharp for tearing; back teeth are flat for chewing.
4. Nerves
5. Sweet, sour, salty, bitter
6. The sense of sweet is detected on the tip of the tongue.

Page 60
(A)
1. MI
2. D
3. D
(B)
1. MI
2. D
3. D
(C)
1. D
2. MI
3. D
(D)
1. D
2. D
3. MI

Page 61
(A) 1. Underlined: Latin is an ancient language...
2. Crossed out: Some English words also come from other...
3. Answers will vary.
(B) 1. Underlined: Ceramics is the shaping and heating...
2.Crossed out: Native

American pottery is among...
3. Answers will vary.

Page 62
Main idea: But this day was...
1. Washington state
2. Earthquake
3. Volcano
4. 123 years
5. They'd been warned.

Page 63
1. Answers will vary.
2. to relieve his boredom; he was amused; a wolf had come
3. They didn't believe him.
4. aid   dull
   tending   amused
   forest   rushing
5. Answers will vary.

Page 64
1. 2 nights
2. $15
3. 4 months
4. $75
5. a. Part of the cost would be wasted.
b. A baby would not appreciate some of the activities.
6. Answers will vary.

Page 65
Main idea: Rattlesnakes are among...
1. True
2. True
3. Doesn't say
4. Doesn't say
5. True
6. False
7. True
8. Doesn't say

Page 66
Answers will vary.

Page 67
I. A President
   C.
      1. Command armed forces
      3. Set foreign policy
      4. Veto laws from Congress
II. Legislative Branch
   B. Represents general population

C.
  2. Impeach the President
  4. Declare war
III A. Supreme Court
  C. Main powers of Judicial Branch
    2. Declare laws unconstitutional

Page 68
A. The ideology difference that developed between Russia and the U.S. after WWII. U.S. and Russia; one in which no shots were fired.
Answers will vary.
B. Louisana Purchase; Sold by Napoleon (France), and purchased by Jefferson (U.S.); 828,000 square miles, from Canada to the Gulf of Mexico.
Answers will vary.

Page 69
Who: Kim and Cho
What: Cho asked Kim for help. Kim tried to trick Cho, but ended up depending on him.
Where: China
When: 1,000 years ago
Why: Kim was greedy and didn't want to see Cho succeed.
Answers will vary.

Page 70
1. General fact
2. General opinion
3. General fact
4. Specific opinion
5. General fact
6. General opinion
7. General opinion
8. General fact
9. Specific fact
10. General fact
11. Specific fact
12. Specific opinion

Page 71
A. People enjoy living in different types of climates.
B. Some plants make their own food; others do not.
C. Porcelain and earthenware are two types of pottery…

Page 72
1. Chicago, Miami
2. Colorado
3. 7
4. Tampa Bay
5. Miami
6. 8
7. San Jose, Columbus
8. Western, Central
9. This is because of the way points are awarded.

Page 73
1. South Carolina
2. Yes
3. Arkansas, Tennessee, Virginia
4. 11
5. Dispute of the economics of and views about slavery.
Answers will vary.

Page 74
  1. 1
  2. nothing
  3. yes
  4. yes
  5. on the curb
  6. 8 am
  7. rinse
  8. could blow around
  9. both
  10. city of Rosewood 389-2341

Page 75
1. pattern of weather over a long time
2. warm/rainy-rains all year; wet/dry has a rainy season
3. tropical
4. amount of precipitation
5. very light precipitation
6. a. polar
b. desert
c. rainy/tropical
d. wet and dry/seasonal

Page 76
Pinniped: southern elephant seal
Bat: western pipistrelle
Fish: whale shark
Deer: southern pudu
Primate: male eastern lowland gorilla
Bird: male bee hummingbird
Snake: reticulated python

Page 77
1. c
2. a
3. d
4. b
5. c

Page 78
1. True
2. False
3. True
4. False
5. True
6. Can't tell
7. True
8. True

Page 79
1. NG
2. G
3. G
4. NG
5. G
6. NG
7. NG

Page 80
The Komodo dragon is the largest…
It exists today only on a few…
This great reptile can…
It has a long tail and…
The Komodo dragon has sharp…
Its size, strength, and powerful…
Komodo dragons hunt during…
This species is a member of…

Page 81
1. fable
2. Answer will vary.
Teaches a lesson or moral value.
3. Doesn't explain forces of nature; doesn't have supernatural beings; not about a person or hero
4. Many things are easier said than done

Page 82
1. mystery
2. fantasy
3. historical fiction
4. realistic fiction
5. realistic fiction
6. science fiction

Page 83
1. historical fiction
2. folklore/fairy tale
3. realistic fiction
4. folklore/myth
5. fantasy
6. science fiction
7. folklore/fable
8. folklore/tall tale
9. mystery
10. folklore/legend
Answers will vary.

Page 84
(A)
1. SS
2. TS
3. SS
(B)
1. TS
2. SS
3. SS
(C)
1. SS
2. SS
3. TS
(D)
1. TS
2. SS
3. SS

Page 85
  1. topic sentence
  2. supporting sentence
  3. topic sentence
  4. topic sentence
  5. supporting sentence
  6. supporting sentence
  7. supporting sentence
  8. topic sentence
  9. supporting sentence
  10. topic sentence
  11. supporting sentence
  12. supporting sentence

Page 86
(Written under paragraph 1)
Their feet are well adapted…
They can carry people and supplies…
(Written under paragraph 2)
The Arabian camel has one hump…
The humps are stores of fat…
The humps enable camels…

Page 87
1. There have been forms of lamps since prehistoric times.
2. Animal fat

3. Story doesn't say
4. Whale oil
5. 1879
6. story doesn't say

Page 88
1. Ramses II
2. Tutankhamen
3. Tutankhamen
4. Coffin
5. Both
6. Bible
7. Ramses II

Page 89
Answers will vary.

Page 90
1. no
2. cough and congestion syrup
3. Answers may vary.
4. Different
5. Cough syrup is "maximum strength", cough lozenges are "regular strength"
6. Syrup/every 6 hours, lozenges/every 2 hours
7. They are alike in that they suggest consulting a doctor; symptoms are different.
8. Answers will vary.

Page 91
1. whale
2. shark
3. both
4. shark
5. shark
6. neither
7. whale
8. shark
9. whale
10. neither
11. whale
12. shark
13. shark

Page 92
Answers will vary.

Page 93
Answers will vary.

Page 94
1. They both like the position they are in.
2-6 Answers will vary.

Page 95
1. she was absent from school today.
2. he checks the

ingredients in what he eats.
3. He apologized to his friend.
4. He takes the stairs instead of the elevator.
5. She stayed after school for some extra help.
6. She borrowed some from a friend.

Page 96

5. Answers will vary.
6. The school could be infested with rats or mice.
7. She knew what it was.
8. A hamster that had escaped.

Page 97

Page 98
Answers will vary.

Page 99
1. 1919 Planes were used and were not invented until 1903.
2. 1787 The Constitution was signed a few years after U.S. independence.
3. 1858 The Civil War ended slavery, so it had to be prior to 1865.
4. 1962 Had to take place after the first airplane but before the first walk on the moon.

Page 100
Answers will vary.

Page 101
Answers will vary.

Page 102
Answers will vary

depending on students' opinions.

Page 103
1. talent show
2. family field day
3. first graders
4. fifth and sixth
5. bake sale 52; sell toys 81; field day 84; talent show 73; spaghetti dinner 74
6-9 Answers will vary.

Page 104
(Sentences checked)
The woman is creating a sculpture.
She is using a power-assisted chisel.
The woman is wearing…
She is concentrating…
Safety goggles protect her…

Page 105
1. sixth; The writer lives on the top floor of a six-story building.
2. girl; The story refer to the best friend as "her"..
3. Chicago, Illinois; The story mentions snow and it does not snow in San Diego, California.
4. He or she likes it.
5. Answers will vary.
6. City; He or she thinks it would be lonely in the suburbs.
Answers will vary.

Page 106
1. sun, planets, satellites, asteroids, comets
2. 1
3. Haley's Comet
4. An asteroid that's entered the earth's atmosphere.
5. Between Jupiter and Mars.

Page 107
1. False
2. True
3. False
4. True
5. False
6. False
7. True
8. False
9. True

10. False

Page 108
1. True
2. False
3. True
4. True
5. False
6. False
7. True
8. True

Page 109
1. True
2. False
3. False
4. True
5. False
6. False
7. True

Page 110
1. told by character
2. told by narrator
3. told by narrator
4. told by narrator
5. told by character
6. told by narrator

Page 111
1. second
2. third
3. second
4. first
5. second

Page 112
1. B, C
2. relax away from work; spend time with the family
3. They're dangerous; Answers will vary.
4-6 Answers will vary.

Page 113
1. a playmate; a dog door
2. She doesn't give him enough attention and treats him like a dog.
3. He's expressing himself.
4. He would stay close by and behave.
5. no
6. better
7. resentful
Answers will vary.

Page 114
1. elephant
2. duck
3. bear

4. frog
5. cat
6. deer
7. chicken
8. alligator
9. monkey
10. horse
11. person
12. ostrich

Page 115
1. Mars
2. meteor
3. the sun
4. Jupiter
5. Pluto
6. Venus
7. Earth's moon
8. Saturn

Page 116
(Correct order)
7, 1, 5, 4, 6, 3, 2

Page 117
Answers: 5, 4, 2, 3, 1
1. Who were the first to make a drink from cacao?
2. Why might the Spanish substituted sugar for spices and peppers?
3. When were the first chocolate bars created?

Page 118
Check to see the colored circle graph represents times suggested.

Page 119
1. sad
2. happy
3. serious
4. silly

Page 120
1. Answers will vary.
2. Answers will vary.
3. A very old (preserved) person; secret life
4. Face like stone and cracked walkway; buckling and weathered skin like sides of house
5. He wasn't sure she'd take them. He might have to take them back.
6. Metaphor
7. Sad and lonely to happy and satisfying

Page 121
Setting: 1814, Switzerland
Main character: Louis
Event #1: wanted to entertain company with his pets; turtles got loose
Event #2: studied animals; became a professor at Harvard
Event #3: student tried to fool him with a practical joke; Louis was not fooled.

Page 122
1. to get reader to figure out what O.T. stands for
2. on time
3. born on his due date
4-5 Answers will vary.

Page 123
1. In some places…
2. Mars is sometimes…
3. Climate is the weather…
4. The U.S. government…
5. All living things…
6. There are distinct differences…

Page 124
1. They were very clever builders—opinion
2. Adobe is pretty and practical.—opinion
3. They also have animals.—irrelevant
4. It would be fun to live on a houseboat.—opinion

Page 125
1. vote for Jackie; She knows how every 7th grade student thinks; Answers will vary.
2. Buy lightening shoes; to be envied by friends; Don't settle for less; these are the best and fastest shoes; Answers will vary

Page 126
Answers will vary.

Page 127
Answers will vary.

Page 128
Answers will vary.

Page 129
Make sure the story of Little Red Riding Hood is in the correct sequence of events.

Page 130
The first auto race.
Ford begins factory with assembly-line production.
Ford spends eight years developing model T.
Ford achieves goal of one car per minute on millionth Model T.
Model T discontinued and other models are developed.

Page 131
Event 1; introduction
Event 2: bragged that she could teach the gods
Event 3: visited and challenged by Athena
Event 4: contest began
Event 5: Athena won
Event 6: Arachne turned into a spider

Page 132
1. Firemen roused by siren.
2. Firemen dress and bolt to trucks.
3. The engine roars to the scene.
4. A boy cries for help.
5. Mac rescues the boy.
6. The building is secure—thanks to the firemen.

Page 133
Answers will vary.

Page 134
Answers will vary.

Page 135
Madison:
Raised a Quaker;
1768-1849;
known for social graces;
saved important documents when British invaded Washington;
place a priority on fashion;
presided at the first inaugural ball
Roosevelt:
1884-1962
was shy and awkward in her youth;
was sensitive to the underprivileged;
was a prolific writer;
served on the UN Human Rights Commission
Both:
First lady;
Among the most admired women of her time;
Was devoted to her husband, the president

Page 136
(Order)
Gerrad sorts mail; gives it to Tanner
Tanner enters invoice and gives to Windley
Windley picks up products and gives them to Hebner
Hebner rechecks everything and sends picklist to Tanner
Tanner adjusts invoice to match shipment
Customer's order and invoice sent out.